# DRUIDIC RESURGENCE: THE MODERN REVIVAL OF AN ANCIENT PATH

### Neo-Druidry and Eco-Spirituality: The Intersection of Past and Present

## D.R. T STEPHENS

**S.D.N Publishing**

While the Druids are most commonly associated with the Celtic peoples of the British Isles and Gaul, their influence and presence were felt throughout the Celtic world.

Celtic society was intricately stratified, and the Druids stood at its apex, commanding respect that transcended tribal boundaries. Their role was not merely spiritual; they wielded considerable power in worldly matters as well. Their decisions could make or break kings, and their blessings were sought for everything from battles to harvests.

## Druidry's Decline and Survival

The coming of the Roman Empire brought cataclysmic changes to the Celtic world, and with it, to the Druids. Roman expansionism and Christianity's ascent marked the beginning of a decline that would see the Druids and their practices pushed to the fringes of society and, eventually, into the shadows of history.

Yet, the essence of Druidry, its deep-rooted connection to the natural world and its cyclical patterns, survived. In the folklore and traditions of the Celtic peoples, the whispers of the ancient Druids endured, carrying the seeds of a spiritual practice that would one day find new soil in which to grow.

## The Historical Tapestry

As historians sift through the layers of time, piecing together the fragments left by classical authors, archaeology, and folklore, a complex picture of the Druids and their world emerges. It is one colored by the biases of their chroniclers, the ravages of time, and the enigmatic nature of the Druids themselves, who committed little of their knowledge to writing. What remains is a tapestry woven from threads of fact, conjecture, and myth, a historical puzzle that continues to challenge and fascinate.

In the end, the origins of Druidry remain partly shrouded in mystery, a fitting beginning for a path that embraces the enigmatic and the sacred. What is undeniable, however, is the profound impact the Druids had on the cultures of their time, and the enduring legacy they have left behind, a legacy that continues to inspire and guide those who seek to walk the Druidic path in the modern world.

We conclude not with an end, but with an invitation to step deeper into the verdant grove of Druidic history and practice, where ancient roots reach into the present, and the whispers of the past guide the footsteps of those who seek the wisdom of the Druids.

# CHAPTER 1: A FORAY INTO DRUIDRY

Welcome, dear seeker, to a realm where ancient wisdom whispers through the leaves, and echoes of a time long past still reverberate in the sacred groves of the present. This is not just a journey through the pages of history, but a voyage into the living, breathing essence of Druidry. In this inaugural chapter, we embark on a friendly foray into the world of Druids, unraveling its mysteries and understanding its relevance in our contemporary tapestry.

## The Roots of Druidry

Druidry, often enshrouded in the mists of time, traces its origins back to the pre-Christian societies of Western Europe. The Druids were the learned class of the Celtic societies, revered as priests, teachers, and custodians of wisdom. However, much of what we know is pieced together from fragments—Roman accounts, archaeological findings, and the rich oral traditions that have survived the relentless march of time.

Contrary to popular belief, the ancient Druids left no written records. Theirs was an oral tradition, woven into the fabric of songs and stories, passed down through generations. This has shrouded their practices in a veil of mystery, allowing mythology to intertwine with what little history we can glean from external sources.

# CHAPTER 2: CORE BELIEFS OF ANCIENT DRUIDS

The ancient Druids, enigmatic figures shrouded in the mists of time, have long captured the imagination of historians and spiritual seekers alike. Their beliefs, intricately woven into the fabric of Celtic society, form a rich tapestry of spiritual, philosophical, and natural principles that continue to influence modern Neo-Druidry. As we delve deeper into their world, it is essential to understand the foundational beliefs that underpinned their practices and how these beliefs harmonized with the natural world they revered.

## Nature and the Divine Immanence

Central to the Druidic worldview was an inextricable connection to nature. The ancient Druids saw divinity not as a distant, detached entity, but as an immanent force that permeated every aspect of the natural world. This pantheistic perspective recognized the sacredness in all things, from the mightiest oak to the smallest stream. The natural world was not merely a backdrop for human activity but a living, breathing manifestation of the divine. It was a source of wisdom, guidance, and spiritual sustenance. Through their intimate relationship with the land, the ancient Druids developed a profound understanding of the cycles of life, death, and rebirth, which were mirrored in the changing seasons and the rhythms of the natural world.

## The Triad of Knowledge, Wisdom, and Truth

Druidic philosophy placed a high value on the pursuit of knowledge, wisdom, and truth. The Druids were the learned class of Celtic society, acting as advisors, jurists, and teachers. They believed that true understanding came from an amalgamation of intellectual pursuit, experiential learning, and inner reflection. Knowledge was not confined to the intellectual realm but extended to a deep, intuitive understanding of the mysteries of the universe. Wisdom, the application of knowledge, was considered essential for maintaining balance and harmony within the self and the community. Truth, an unwavering principle, was to be sought relentlessly, even when shrouded in ambiguity and paradox.

## The Sanctity of Oral Tradition and Memory

In the absence of written records, the Druids relied on a rich oral tradition to pass down their lore, history, and wisdom. Memory was revered, and the power of the spoken word was paramount. Bards, a subset of the Druidic class, were the custodians of these oral traditions, using poetry, song, and story to preserve and transmit knowledge. This reverence for the spoken word elevated language to a sacred art form, believed to hold intrinsic power and magic. The meticulous memorization and recitation of lore ensured that each generation remained connected to the past, forming a continuous thread of collective memory and identity.

## The Interconnectedness of All Life

The ancient Druids perceived a profound interconnectedness

between all forms of life. This belief in the unity of existence extended beyond the physical realm to encompass the spiritual and ethereal. The concept of the Otherworld, a parallel dimension intertwined with the physical world, was a testament to this interconnectedness. The Druids believed that the veil between the worlds was permeable, and significant times of the year, such as the festivals of Samhain and Beltane, provided opportunities for communication and interaction with the Otherworld. This holistic worldview fostered a deep sense of responsibility and stewardship towards the land, the community, and the cosmos.

## The Ethical Framework: Honor, Courage, and Integrity

Ethical conduct was a cornerstone of Druidic belief. Honor, courage, and integrity were not mere virtues but essential components of one's character. The Druids upheld a moral code that emphasized the importance of living in harmony with others and the natural world. Honor involved maintaining one's reputation through righteous actions, courage was the strength to face adversity and uphold one's convictions, and integrity required unwavering adherence to truth and moral principles. This ethical framework guided individual behavior and societal norms, ensuring that the community functioned cohesively and justly.

As we unravel the core beliefs of the ancient Druids, we begin to understand the profound reverence they held for the natural world, the importance they placed on knowledge and wisdom, and the ethical principles that guided their lives. These foundational beliefs, though ancient, continue to resonate with modern seekers, providing a timeless framework for understanding our place in the world and our relationship with the divine. As we continue our exploration of Druidry, we carry with us the wisdom of the ancients, a wisdom that remains as relevant today as it was millennia ago.

## Modern Druidry: A New Dawn

As the morning sun crests the horizon and bathes ancient stone circles in its warming glow, it also ushers in a new dawn for a tradition steeped in mystery and reverence for the natural world. Modern Druidry, a resurgence of an age-old path, is not merely a revival of ancient practices but an evolving spiritual movement that resonates deeply with the challenges and sensibilities of contemporary life.

## The Roots Reimagined

Modern Druidry, often referred to as Neo-Druidry, draws its essence from the rich soil of ancient Druidic tradition, yet it is not confined by it. This modern iteration is not a rigid replica of the past but a living, breathing adaptation that respects its origins while innovatively responding to the present. One could liken it to an ancient language that has evolved over centuries, its core unchanged but its expression adapted to the modern tongue.

The ancient Druids were revered for their wisdom, spiritual insight, and deep connection with the natural world. They served as advisors, healers, and mediators, holding esteemed positions in their societies. Today's Druids aspire to emulate these roles in a contemporary context, serving as stewards of the earth, seekers of wisdom, and advocates for peace and harmony.

## Diversity in Modern Druidry

The beauty of modern Druidry lies in its diversity and inclusivity. Unlike the structured hierarchies and dogmas that characterize many spiritual paths, Druidry in its current form is fluid, allowing practitioners the freedom to shape their practice according to their personal beliefs and experiences. This openness has fostered a vibrant tapestry of interpretations and expressions, from those who strictly adhere to historical reconstructions to those who blend Druidic practices with other spiritual paths, creating a rich and diverse spiritual ecosystem.

Modern Druidic organizations and orders, such as the Order of Bards, Ovates, and Druids (OBOD) and Ár nDraíocht Féin (ADF), offer structured paths of study and community for those seeking guidance and fellowship. However, many choose a solitary path, finding solace and connection in their individual practices. Whether in a grove or alone beneath the canopy of stars, the spirit of Druidry thrives in the hearts of its followers.

## Embracing the Modern World

Modern Druids are not anachronisms, yearning for a return to bygone days; they are fully engaged with the world around them. They embrace modern technology and science, viewing them as tools that, when used responsibly, can enhance their understanding of the universe and aid in the stewardship of the Earth. For instance, they may use social media to connect with like-minded individuals across the globe or employ scientific knowledge in their ecological endeavors, bridging the ancient and the contemporary in a harmonious dance.

One of the most compelling aspects of modern Druidry is its emphasis on ecological responsibility and sustainability. As the world grapples with environmental challenges, the Druidic reverence for nature and its cycles offers a profound framework for understanding and addressing these issues. Modern Druids often find themselves at the forefront of ecological activism, drawing from their spiritual beliefs to advocate for the preservation and healing of the planet.

Modern Druidry is not a relic but a renaissance, a tradition reborn and reimagined for the contemporary seeker. It honors its roots while branching out to embrace the complexities and challenges of the modern world.

# CHAPTER 3: THE PANTHEON OF CELTIC DEITIES

In the druidic tradition, a profound connection to the natural world is paralleled by a rich tapestry of deities, each embodying elemental forces, natural phenomena, and human endeavors. These gods and goddesses form the heart of the Celtic pantheon, revered not only for their divine might but also for their intimate intertwining with the lives of those who worship them. The druidic path often involves cultivating relationships with these deities, understanding their archetypes, and honoring their presence within the natural world and the self.

## Deities of Land, Sea, and Sky

The Celtic pantheon is characterized by its variety and complexity, with gods and goddesses representing the land, sea, and sky. Among them, Danu is often revered as the primordial mother, a figure of fertility and abundance, embodying the Earth itself. Her children, the Tuatha Dé Danann, are a race of deities whose stories weave through Irish mythology, each member possessing unique attributes and responsibilities.

The sea, a domain of both bounty and mystery, is personified by Manannán mac Lir, a deity of the Otherworld who navigates the ethereal mists between realms. His is a presence felt in the pull of tides and the whispers of sea-spray, a guardian of the threshold between worlds.

In contrast, the sky is the domain of the thunderous Taranis, whose voice reverberates in the crash of thunder and whose power flashes in the strike of lightning. His is a force both destructive and life-giving, a reminder of the raw, untamed energy that suffuses the world.

## The Cycle of Life and Death

The rhythm of life and death holds a central place in Celtic belief systems, embodied by deities who represent these cyclical forces. The Morrígan, a complex figure often seen as a triad of goddesses, presides over war, fate, and sovereignty. Her presence is that of the raven, the carrion bird that follows in the wake of battle, and the prophetess who foresees the threads of destiny.

Contrasting the Morrígan is Brigid, a goddess of healing, poetry, and smithcraft. She ushers in the spring, her flame a beacon of rebirth and renewal. Her dual aspect as both a nurturing mother and a fierce protector encapsulates the interplay of creation and preservation.

## Guardians of Craft and Skill

Druidry also venerates deities of skill and craft, recognizing the divine in human endeavors. Lugh, known as the master of all arts, embodies excellence and versatility. His prowess is not confined to battle alone; he is a patron of craftspeople, artists, and healers alike, symbolizing the pursuit of mastery in all forms.

Similarly, Ogma, credited with the invention of the Ogham script, represents wisdom and eloquence. His is the power of the spoken word, the enchantment that lies in tales well told and knowledge carefully preserved.

## Harmonizing with the Divine

Engaging with the pantheon is more than an act of reverence; it is a process of harmonizing one's own spirit with the divine. Druidic practices often involve meditation, ritual, and contemplation designed to forge connections with these deities. By aligning oneself with the attributes of a particular god or goddess, adherents seek to embody their qualities, finding guidance and inspiration in their ancient myths and stories.

These deities are not seen as distant, omnipotent figures but as accessible, relational beings whose energies pervade the natural world. In honoring them, one honors the forces they represent —the fertility of the earth, the depth of the sea, the expanse of the sky, and the intricate dance of life and death. Through ritual, celebration, and mindful living, druids seek to become attuned to these divine energies, weaving them into the fabric of their daily lives.

From the primordial energies of land, sea, and sky to the intricate dance of life and death, each deity embodies fundamental aspects of existence. As we continue our exploration of Druidry, these gods and goddesses will serve as touchstones, guiding us deeper into the heart of this ancient path.

## The Wheel of the Year: Druidic Festivals

In the tapestry of modern Druidry, the Wheel of the Year holds a position of considerable reverence and significance. This cyclical calendar marks the passage of the seasons through eight festivals, each brimming with symbolic import and rich in ritual. These festivals serve not only as a homage to the natural rhythms of the Earth but also as spiritual milestones that guide the practitioner through a journey of perpetual renewal and transformation.

## The Festivals of the Wheel

The Wheel of the Year is segmented into eight festivals, with each festivity embodying a unique facet of the Druidic understanding of time and nature. These festivals are not merely commemorations but are seen as living, breathing events that invite participants to immerse themselves in the ebb and flow of the natural world.

**Samhain (October 31st - November 1st):** Often considered the Druidic New Year, Samhain marks the end of the harvest season and the beginning of winter. It is a time of reflection, remembrance, and honoring the ancestors. The veil between worlds is believed to be thinnest on this night, facilitating communion with the spirits.

**Yule (Winter Solstice, around December 21st):** Celebrating the rebirth of the Sun, Yule is a festival of light in the deepest darkness of winter. It is a time of hope and renewal, as the days begin to lengthen once again.

**Imbolc (February 1st - 2nd):** Imbolc heralds the early signs of spring. It is a festival of purification and a celebration of the returning light and life. The goddess Brigid is often honored during this time, symbolizing fertility, healing, and poetry.

**Ostara (Spring Equinox, around March 21st):** The balance of day and night at the Equinox brings the promise of fertility and growth. Ostara is a celebration of this equilibrium and the burgeoning life that spring brings forth.

**Beltane (May 1st):** This festival ignites the fires of creativity and passion. Beltane marks the height of spring and the beginning of summer. It is a time of fertility, sensuality, and the vibrant interplay of masculine and feminine energies.

**Litha (Summer Solstice, around June 21st):** At the peak of the Sun's power, Litha is a celebration of light and abundance. It is a time to rejoice in the fullness of life and to acknowledge the nurturing warmth of the Sun.

**Lughnasadh or Lammas (August 1st):** As the first of the harvest festivals, Lughnasadh is a time of gratitude for the bounties of the Earth. It is also a time of sacrifice, as the Sun begins to wane and the days grow shorter.

**Mabon (Autumn Equinox, around September 21st):** The second harvest festival, Mabon, is a time of balance and reflection. As day and night hold equal sway, it is a period for giving thanks and preparing for the darker half of the year.

## Rituals and Celebrations

Each festival is marked by specific rituals and customs that deepen the connection between the practitioner and the natural world. These rituals often involve elements such as fire, which symbolizes transformation and renewal, and water, which signifies purification and healing. Chants, songs, and dances are also integral, serving as means to harmonize with the rhythms of nature and to express joy, gratitude, and reverence.

At Samhain, for instance, a common ritual involves setting an extra place at the table to honor the ancestors, while at Beltane, the maypole dance weaves participants together in a tapestry of unity and festivity. Yule logs are burned to welcome the return of the Sun, and at Imbolc, candles are lit to represent the growing light.

## The Wheel and the Modern Druid

In contemporary Druidry, the Wheel of the Year serves as a powerful tool for self-reflection and spiritual growth. Each festival presents an opportunity to align with the natural cycles and to draw lessons from the Earth's transformations. The cyclical nature of the Wheel teaches the importance of balance, resilience, and the beauty of impermanence.

The festivals also foster a sense of community as practitioners gather to celebrate, often in groves or other natural settings, strengthening their bond with each other and with the Earth. In an increasingly disconnected world, these celebrations offer a touchstone, grounding individuals in the rhythms of nature and the communal spirit of the Druidic path.

The Wheel of the Year forms a core component of Druidic practice, encapsulating the cyclical and interconnected nature of life. Through the observance of its festivals, modern Druids not only honor the traditions of their ancestors but also cultivate a deep, living relationship with the natural world and its ever-unfolding mysteries.

# CHAPTER 4: SACRED SITES AND THEIR SIGNIFICANCE

In the verdant embrace of nature, enshrined in the quietude of forest glades and the mystical silence of stone circles, lie the sacred sites of Druidry. These are places where the veil between worlds is thin, where the ancient Druids performed rituals and sought communion with the divine. As we delve into the sanctified grounds of Druidic lore, we begin to comprehend their significance not only in ancient times but also in the contemporary revival of Druidry.

## The Hallowed Groves

To understand the significance of sacred groves in Druidry, one must appreciate the Druidic worldview that perceives divinity in all forms of nature. Sacred groves, often known as 'Nemeton' in the Celtic tongue, served as the cathedrals of the Druids, where natural sanctuaries, untouched by the profanity of axes, became the epicenter of worship and ceremony. In these leafy enclosures, the Druids found solace and connection to the natural world, reinforcing their belief in the interconnectivity of all life. The groves were not merely geographical locations but portals to the spiritual realm, fostering a deeper understanding of the cycles of life, death, and rebirth, evident in the ever-changing seasons.

## The Resonance of Stone Circles

As we transition from the serenity of groves to the enigmatic stone circles that punctuate the landscapes of Britain and Ireland, their purpose extends beyond mere curiosity. These megalithic structures, like the famed Stonehenge or the lesser-known but equally captivating Ring of Brodgar, function as cosmic calculators and celestial observatories. Their precise alignments with solstices, equinoxes, and specific star constellations elucidate their role in marking the Wheel of the Year, a cornerstone of Druidic practice. As the sun's rays pierce through these ancient stones on auspicious days, we are reminded of the continuity of time and the ancient wisdom that sought to harmonize human existence with the greater cosmic dance.

## The Wellsprings of Wisdom

Not all sacred sites are marked by the prominence of towering stones. Springs and wells, often unassuming and tucked away in the quiet recesses of the landscape, held profound spiritual significance for the Druids. These wellsprings, viewed as the abode of deities and the source of curative powers, were frequented for healing, divination, and the veneration of water deities. The practice of 'clootie' trees, where cloths are tied to branches near sacred wells as offerings or petitions for blessings, reflects the enduring legacy of these sites in modern Druidic practice.

As we immerse ourselves in the study of these sacred sites, we uncover layers of symbology, reverence, and cosmic alignment that are integral to Druidic belief. While these sites serve as conduits to the past, their enduring legacy in modern Druidry is a testament to the unbroken thread of spirituality that connects us to our ancestors. They remind us of the sanctity of the natural world and the enduring human quest for understanding our place within it.

The sacred sites of Druidry, encompassing groves, stone circles, and wells, are more than mere points on a map. They are vibrant loci of spiritual energy and historical continuity, informing and enriching the modern Druidic path. As we explore these sanctified grounds, we tread the footsteps of the ancients, seeking wisdom and connection in the sacred embrace of the Earth.

## The Bardic Tradition

In the intricately woven tapestry of Druidic culture, the bards held a position of reverence and significance. Their role transcended mere entertainment; bards were the custodians of memory and the messengers of the mystical. Their poetry and stories were not just art—they were conduits of wisdom, history, and cultural identity.

## The Historical Bard

In ancient Druidic society, the bard was more than a mere poet or musician; they were the bearers of culture, the scribes of the oral tradition. The bard's task was to memorize vast compendiums of lore and history, encapsulating the struggles and triumphs of their people through epic poems and songs. Their works were not merely recitations of facts; they were imbued with allegory, metaphor, and spiritual significance, often intertwined with the cosmology and mythos of the Druids.

Training to become a bard was a rigorous and demanding journey, often taking upwards of a decade or more. Aspirants would learn not only the intricacies of language and meter but also the subtleties of performance. To be a bard was to hold a mirror to the soul of society, reflecting its deepest values, fears, and aspirations.

## Bards in Modern Druidry

In contemporary Druidry, the bardic tradition has undergone a renaissance. Modern bards are still the storytellers, poets, and musicians, but their role has expanded to include various forms of artistic expression. They are painters, sculptors, and dancers, each contributing to the rich tapestry of modern Druidic life.

For modern Druids, the bardic arts are not confined to the retelling of ancient tales; they are also a means of engaging with the present. Bards create works that reflect current societal challenges, weave tales that inspire ecological stewardship, and compose music that resonates with the frequency of the natural world. They are not mere entertainers; they are catalysts for reflection, introspection, and communal unity.

## The Spiritual Aspect of Bardism

At its core, the bardic tradition in Druidry is deeply spiritual. It recognizes the divine essence that permeates all forms of art. Whether it is the cadence of a well-crafted poem, the melody of a haunting tune, or the vibrant strokes of a painted landscape, each is seen as an expression of the Awen—the divine inspiration central to Druidic belief.

The Awen flows through the bard, enabling them to transform the mundane into the sublime. Their creations are not just for the pleasure of the senses; they are vehicles for spiritual awakening and growth. Through their art, bards can elicit profound emotional responses, stir the soul, and awaken a deeper connection to the natural world and the ineffable mysteries of existence.

The bardic tradition is a testament to the enduring human need for storytelling, creative expression, and the communion of shared experiences. In Druidry, this tradition is not a relic of the past but a vibrant and evolving practice. The modern bard bridges the gap between the ancient and the contemporary, between the human and the divine, weaving tales and creating art that both honors the legacy of their ancestors and speaks to the heart of the present moment.

As we journey deeper into the world of Druidry, the bardic tradition stands as a beacon, reminding us that art is not just decoration but a profound expression of the human spirit, a reflection of our deepest truths, and a portal to the divine.

# CHAPTER 5: DRUIDIC SYMBOLS AND THEIR MEANINGS

Symbols serve as the shorthand of the soul, a visual lexicon capable of conveying layers of meaning and ancient wisdom in a single glance. In the realm of Druidry, symbols are not mere representations; they are conduits of power, mystery, and connection to the natural world and its rhythms. Let's delve into the mystique of Druidic symbols, unraveling their meanings, origins, and their enduring significance in the practice of modern Druidry.

## The Awen: The Flow of Inspiration

Central to Druidic symbology is the Awen, often depicted as three rays of light emanating from three points of light or as three dots with rays descending from them. The term "Awen" in the Gaelic language translates to "inspiration" or "essence," capturing the core of Druidic practice — the quest for spiritual inspiration and enlightenment. The three rays represent harmony, balance, and the unity of opposites, embodying the Druidic belief in the interconnectedness of all things. They are also seen as a symbol of the triad of the mind, body, and spirit, which must be in equilibrium for one to live a fulfilling life.

The Awen is not just a symbol but a state of being, sought after in meditation and ritual. It represents the divine spark of creativity and insight that Druids strive to ignite within themselves. It is a reminder of the ever-present flow of the spirit of the universe, offering wisdom, poetic inspiration, and a deeper understanding of the natural world.

## Ogham: The Mysterious Tree Alphabet

Another cornerstone of Druidic symbolism is Ogham, an ancient writing system often referred to as the "Celtic Tree Alphabet." Each character or "fid" in Ogham corresponds to a particular tree or plant, each bearing its own unique spiritual significance and essence. For example, Birch, the first tree in the Ogham, symbolizes new beginnings and purification, while Oak, the king of trees, signifies strength, stability, and nobility.

Ogham is not merely an alphabet but a sacred system of knowledge and divination. Each tree's attributes are thought to carry messages and wisdom from the natural world. Ogham is deeply entwined with the Druidic reverence for trees as living, spiritual entities. The practice of Ogham divination involves casting sticks or stones inscribed with the symbols and interpreting the patterns and relationships they form when they fall.

## The Triskele: The Spiral of Continuity

The Triskele, or triple spiral, is a motif that appears frequently in Celtic and Druidic art. Its three spirals are believed to represent a variety of triads, such as land, sea, and sky; past, present, and future; or creation, preservation, and destruction. Like the Awen, it embodies the principle of threes, a sacred number in Druidry.

The Triskele is a symbol of motion, progress, and the cyclical nature of life. Its spirals evoke the continuous flow and progression of time and the seasons. It also resonates with the concept of reincarnation, a belief held by some Druids, reflecting the soul's journey through various forms and lifetimes.

## The Green Man: The Face of Nature

The Green Man is an enigmatic figure found in many cultures but is particularly associated with Celtic and Druidic traditions. Typically depicted as a face surrounded by or made of leaves, the Green Man symbolizes the union of humanity and nature, the life force that flows through the natural world.

He is a reminder of the cycles of growth and decay, of the eternal rebirth of nature in the spring after the death of winter. The Green Man is both ancient and ever-new, embodying the resilience and endless creativity of nature.

## Symbolism in Modern Druidry

In contemporary Druidry, these symbols and others continue to play a vital role. They adorn altars, jewelry, and ritual tools, serving as touchstones for meditation and sources of insight. They are not relics of a bygone era but living symbols, evolving and accruing new layers of meaning as Druids engage with them in their practices.

These symbols bridge the gap between ancient wisdom and modern experience, providing a means of accessing and expressing the ineffable — that which lies beyond the reach of words. In the hands of modern Druids, they are keys to unlocking the mysteries of the self and the cosmos.

Druidic symbols like the Awen, Ogham, Triskele, and the Green Man are more than mere marks or glyphs. They are potent tools for spiritual exploration and growth, weaving together the past and present, the human and the divine, the material and the ethereal. They beckon practitioners to delve deeper into the mysteries of Druidry, guiding them on a path strewn with the rich tapestry of Celtic spirituality and wisdom.

## Nature and the Druidic Path

The Druidic tradition is deeply rooted in the natural world, seeing it not merely as a resource to be exploited, but as a sacred, living tapestry of which humans are an integral part. Let's delve into the symbiotic relationship between Druidry and nature, exploring how this ancient path sees the natural world, interacts with it, and draws spiritual nourishment from it.

## The Living Cosmos

In the Druidic worldview, nature is not inanimate or passive. It is a dynamic, living cosmos brimming with spirits, energies, and consciousness. Trees, rivers, stones, and mountains are not seen as mere physical objects, but as living entities with spirits. This animistic perspective is fundamental to Druidic practice, which often involves communicating with and honoring these natural spirits.

For Druids, every aspect of the natural world is infused with the divine. The sun, moon, and stars are not distant celestial bodies but are imbued with spiritual significance. Celestial events like solstices and equinoxes are not just astronomical occurrences but are sacred times of power and reflection. The phases of the moon guide rituals and magical workings, acknowledging the moon's influence on the natural world and the human psyche.

## Sacred Interactions

Druidic practice involves a respectful and reciprocal relationship with nature. It's not a one-sided affair where humans take what they need without giving back. Instead, Druids seek to live in harmony with the natural world, taking only what is needed and offering gratitude and blessings in return. This can involve rituals of offering, such as pouring libations onto the earth or leaving biodegradable tokens of appreciation in sacred groves.

This reciprocity extends to environmental stewardship. Modern Druids often engage in ecological activism and land conservation, seeing this as part of their spiritual duty. The health of the natural world is directly tied to the spiritual wellbeing of the Druid, and so protecting and restoring nature is a sacred task.

## Nature as Teacher

In Druidry, nature is not just a place to live; it is a source of wisdom and learning. Druids believe that by observing the rhythms and patterns of nature, one can gain insights into the mysteries of life and the cosmos. The changing seasons teach about the cycles of birth, growth, decay, and rebirth. Animal behaviors provide lessons in adaptation and survival. Even the patterns of leaves and the flow of rivers can hold profound spiritual lessons for those attuned to nature's subtleties.

This aspect of Druidry involves spending time in nature, not just passively enjoying its beauty, but actively engaging with it. Walking in the woods, sitting by a stream, or simply being present in a garden can be acts of spiritual communion and learning.

## The Healing Power of Nature

Druids also recognize the therapeutic benefits of nature. Modern psychology has begun to acknowledge what Druids have long known: that spending time in natural settings can have significant positive effects on mental health. This concept, often referred to as "eco-therapy" or "forest bathing" in contemporary terms, is a vital component of the Druidic path.

For Druids, the healing power of nature goes beyond stress reduction or mood enhancement. It is a form of deep, spiritual healing that involves realigning the soul with the natural rhythms of the earth. This can involve meditative practices in nature, herbalism, or energy work at sacred sites.

The relationship between Druidry and nature is profound and integral. It is a symbiotic bond that nourishes both the Druid and the natural world. By understanding and embracing this connection, one can step onto a path of harmony, wisdom, and spiritual fulfillment. In a world where the disconnection from nature is all too common, the Druidic perspective offers a healing and transformative vision, one where humans and nature exist in respectful, sacred communion.

# CHAPTER 6: THE ROLE OF MAGIC IN DRUIDRY

In the realm of Druidry, the concept of magic transcends mere illusion or sleight of hand; it is a profound and intricate facet of the spiritual path. To understand Druidic magic, one must first appreciate that it is deeply rooted in a profound reverence for nature and its inherent powers. The aim is to elucidate the contours of magic within Druidry, exploring its significance, practices, and the philosophical underpinnings that render it an indispensable element of this ancient yet ever-evolving path.

## The Essence of Druidic Magic

At its core, Druidic magic is about connection. It is the ethereal thread that weaves together the practitioner with the cosmos, the earth, and all living entities. This interconnectedness is foundational to Druidic belief and practice, and magic is the means by which Druids engage with these connections in a deliberate and profound way. It is a practice that honors the belief that every stone, plant, animal, and breath of wind possesses a spirit—a life force that can be interacted with and respected.

## Practices and Rituals

Druidic magic is not a monolithic construct; it is a tapestry of varied practices and rituals, each resonating with the vibrations of the natural world. These practices include, but are not limited to:

**Visualization and Meditation:** Druids harness the power of their mind's eye to envisage outcomes, connect with spiritual entities, or attune themselves to the energies of the earth. Meditation serves as a vessel for grounding and centering, essential for any magical working.

**Nature Immersion:** Embracing the sanctity of nature, Druids often perform rituals in sacred groves or near ancient trees, drawing on the potent energies of these spaces. The belief is that nature is not merely a backdrop but an active participant in the magical process.

**Incantation and Chanting:** Words are wielded with precision and intent in Druidic magic. Chants, often in the form of poems or songs, are used to raise energy, invoke deities, or manifest desires. The vibration of sound is a potent force within Druidic practices.

**Symbolic Gestures:** Druidic rituals are rich with symbolic actions, such as the casting of a circle to create sacred space, or the anointing of the forehead with water from a sacred spring. Each gesture is laden with meaning and intent.

**Divination:** Druids engage with various forms of divination, such as reading Ogham staves or observing the flight patterns of birds, to gain insights, seek guidance, or understand the will of the divine.

## Philosophical Foundations

The philosophy underpinning Druidic magic is as rich and diverse as the practices themselves. A key principle is the belief in the animistic nature of the universe—that everything has a spirit and a consciousness. This belief necessitates a respectful approach to magic, where the practitioner seeks harmony and balance rather than domination or control.

Another significant philosophical aspect is the concept of *Wyrd*, often understood as a web of fate or destiny. Druids perceive their magical workings as interactions with this web, understanding that each action can have far-reaching consequences, thus emphasizing the importance of ethical considerations in magical practice.

Magic in Druidry is not an arcane relic of the past but a vibrant and living practice that continues to evolve and adapt. It is a testament to the Druidic path's reverence for nature and its dedication to harmony and balance. Through the practices and philosophies of Druidic magic, practitioners find a profound connection to the world around them, a connection that enriches their spiritual journey and fosters a deep sense of unity with the cosmos.

## Rituals and Rites of Passage

In the verdant fabric of Druidry, rituals and rites of passage stand as threads that weave the past and present into a continuous tapestry of spiritual practice. These ceremonies, rich in symbolism and steeped in tradition, are the milestones and markers of a Druid's path, guiding practitioners through the seasons of the year and the seasons of life. Let's endeavor to elucidate the quintessence of these ceremonies, unraveling their significance and the transformative power they hold in the journey of a modern Druid.

## The Essence of Druidic Rituals

At the heart of Druidry, rituals are more than mere formalities; they are a profound communion with the natural world, the ancestors, and the pantheon of Celtic deities. These ceremonies, whether celebrated solitarily or communally, serve as a nexus point between the mundane and the sacred, opening portals to higher consciousness and facilitating a deepened understanding of one's place in the cosmos.

Rituals in Druidry are often conducted within the sanctity of nature, in groves that whisper ancient secrets or by standing stones that have borne witness to the passage of aeons. Here, the Druid engages in a series of symbolic acts, from the lighting of candles and the offering of libations to the chanting of invocations and the casting of circles. Each gesture is imbued with intention, transforming the ritual into an alchemical process that transmutes the spiritual seeker.

## Rites of Passage: Celebrating Life's Transitions

In the undulating journey of life, Druidry recognizes and honors the pivotal transitions that shape our existence. From birth to death, these rites of passage are celebrated with reverence and ritual, each tailored to mark the significance of the milestone it represents.

## Birth and Naming Ceremonies

In welcoming a new soul into the world, Druids conduct naming ceremonies, invoking the blessings of the elements and the divine to guide the child's path. These ceremonies are replete with symbols of potential and protection, often incorporating the planting of a tree or the bestowal of a namesake stone, rooting the child in the embrace of nature and the community.

## Coming of Age

The transition from childhood to adulthood is a momentous occasion, marked by a rite of passage that signifies the individual's readiness to assume greater responsibilities within the community. This ceremony often involves a quest or a challenge, a symbolic journey that echoes the hero's odyssey, culminating in the recognition of the young adult's place within the circle of Druids.

## Handfasting and Marriage

Handfasting, the sacred union of two souls, is celebrated with profound joy and solemnity. The ritual, often conducted in the presence of the elements, involves the literal tying of hands with a cord, symbolizing the couple's commitment to intertwining their destinies. This ancient practice, replete with blessings and vows, sanctifies the bond of love and partnership, weaving it into the fabric of the community.

## Death and Passing Over Rites

In the twilight of life, Druids view death not as an end but as a transition to another realm of existence. The passing over rites are conducted with deep respect and compassion, aiding the soul's journey to the Otherworld. These ceremonies often involve a recitation of the individual's achievements, a celebration of their life, and a gentle guiding of their spirit to the ancestors and the divine, ensuring that their essence continues to resonate within the sacred grove of memory.

## The Transformational Power of Ritual

Engaging in Druidic rituals and rites of passage is a transformative experience, one that transcends the boundaries of time and space. These ceremonies serve as a conduit for personal growth, facilitating a profound connection with the self, the community, and the divine. Through the rhythmic cadence of ritual, the Druid is continuously reborn, shedding old skins and embracing new vistas of spiritual understanding.

In the intricate dance of existence, rituals and rites of passage are the steps that lead the Druid through the spirals of life. They are the whispers of the ancestors, the songs of the earth, and the echoes of the divine, harmonizing the individual soul with the symphony of the cosmos. As we continue our journey through the realm of modern Druidry, these ceremonies stand as beacons, illuminating the path of the seeker and imbuing the quest with sacred significance.

# CHAPTER 7: TOOLS OF THE DRUID

In the world of Druidry, tools are more than mere physical objects; they are sacred conduits of energy, symbols of the craft, and extensions of the practitioner's intentions. Let's explore the various tools that are integral to Druidic practices, their symbolism, usage, and the profound connection that Druids establish with these instruments of their ancient art.

**The Wand and Staff: Symbols of Authority and Guidance**

Among the most iconic tools in Druidry are the wand and the staff, each serving a distinct purpose in the Druid's journey. The wand, often crafted from wood associated with specific magical properties, is a tool of invocation and direction. It is used to channel energy, cast circles, and in the directing of spells or intentions. The wood chosen for a wand might vary depending on the purpose for which it is intended; for instance, an oak wand for strength and protection, or a willow wand for healing and emotional work.

The staff, typically longer and sturdier than the wand, is a symbol of the Druid's journey and authority. It represents the world tree, a central concept in many pagan traditions, symbolizing the axis mundi, or the connection between the heavens, earth, and underworld. The staff is a walking companion, a tool for ceremonial use, and in some traditions, a marker of one's progress through the Druidic grades.

## The Cauldron: Vessel of Transformation and Rebirth

The cauldron is a potent symbol within Druidry, representing transformation, rebirth, and the womb of the Goddess. In ritual, it is used for brewing potions, scrying, or as a container for offerings. The cauldron symbolizes the transformative nature of magic, the blending of ingredients to create something new, and the mysteries of the feminine divine. It is a reminder of the ever-present potential for change, growth, and renewal.

## The Druid's Altar: A Sacred Space

The altar is the Druid's sacred workspace, a focal point for rituals, and a personal sanctuary for meditation and reflection. It is often adorned with items that hold personal or spiritual significance, such as crystals, statues of deities, candles, and symbols of the elements. The altar is a microcosm of the Druid's world, reflecting their beliefs, their connection to the natural world, and their spiritual journey.

## The Significance of Personalization

While there are common tools used in Druidic practice, it is the personalization of these tools that imbues them with deeper meaning. Druids are encouraged to craft or find their own tools, infusing them with personal energy and intention. This process creates a bond between the practitioner and the tool, making it a unique extension of their own spiritual essence.

Tools are often consecrated in a ritual, aligning them with the Druid's purpose and energy. This consecration is a sacred act, marking the tool's transition from a mundane object to a key instrument in the Druid's spiritual practice.

The tools of the Druid are more than mere instruments; they are sacred objects, imbued with symbolic meaning and personal significance. They serve as bridges between the physical and spiritual realms, facilitating the practitioner's interaction with the energies of the universe. In the hands of a Druid, these tools become allies in the journey of spiritual exploration, growth, and connection with the natural world.

The tools of Druidry are extensions of the practitioner's will and intention. They are symbols of the ancient path walked by Druids, and each tool holds a key to unlocking deeper layers of meaning and understanding in their spiritual practice. As we continue to explore the rich tapestry of Druidry, these tools stand as reminders of the profound connection between the physical and the spiritual, the practitioner, and the path.

## The Three Grades: Bard, Ovate, and Druid

In the tapestry of modern Druidry, the path is often conceptualized as a journey through three primary grades or roles: Bard, Ovate, and Druid. These grades represent different aspects of learning, spiritual growth, and service within the Druidic tradition. Let's delve into the distinct characteristics of each grade, exploring their historical roots, their roles in contemporary Druidry, and the journey through these stages.

## The Bard: The Keeper of Lore and Art

The first stage in the Druidic path is that of the Bard. Historically, Bards were the poets, musicians, and storytellers of Celtic societies, revered as keepers of lore, history, and ancestral wisdom. In modern Druidry, the Bardic grade is centered around the development of creativity, the study of mythology, folklore, and the arts, and the cultivation of the powers of observation and expression.

Bards are often seen as the custodians of culture and heritage, using their skills in art and language to connect with the ancestral past and to express the sacred in the world around them. Training in the Bardic grade typically involves learning about Celtic mythology, developing artistic skills, engaging with nature through the arts, and exploring the power of storytelling and poetry.

## The Ovate: The Seer and Healer

The second grade in the Druidic path is the Ovate. Ovates are traditionally associated with divination, healing, and working with the mysteries of life and death. This grade delves deeper into the spiritual and esoteric aspects of Druidry, focusing on developing skills in areas such as divination, herbalism, and understanding the cycles of nature.

Ovates are often seen as intermediaries between the physical and spiritual realms, using their knowledge and skills to bring healing and balance. Training for an Ovate may include studying herbal lore, practicing various forms of divination (like Ogham or tarot), engaging in meditation and journeying practices, and exploring the mysteries of birth, death, and rebirth.

## The Druid: The Wise One and Guide

The third and final grade is that of the Druid. This stage is associated with a deeper understanding of philosophy, teaching, counseling, and leadership within the community. Druids are often viewed as wise counselors, spiritual leaders, and keepers of sacred knowledge.

The training and development at this stage involve a deeper exploration of metaphysical concepts, ethical considerations, leadership skills, and the practice of ritual and ceremony. Druids are expected to embody the wisdom of both the Bard and the Ovate, integrating these skills into a comprehensive understanding of the self, the community, and the wider world.

## The Journey Through the Grades

The journey through the grades of Bard, Ovate, and Druid is not merely a process of accumulating knowledge but a transformative spiritual and personal journey. Each grade builds upon the last, guiding the practitioner deeper into the mysteries of Druidry and their own inner landscape. It is a path of continual growth, learning, and service to both the community and the natural world.

While these grades provide a framework for training and development, the journey of each Druid is unique, influenced by their personal experiences, talents, and spiritual calling. The journey through Bard, Ovate, and Druid grades is a lifelong path of discovery, connection, and contribution to the tapestry of Druidry and the world.

The three grades of Bard, Ovate, and Druid offer a structured yet flexible path for those seeking to delve deep into the Druidic tradition. Each grade represents a vital aspect of the Druid's journey, providing a framework for learning, growth, and service within the ancient yet ever-evolving path of Druidry.

# CHAPTER 8: DRUIDRY AND OTHER PAGAN PATHS

In the diverse tapestry of contemporary spirituality, Druidry often intertwines and overlaps with various other Pagan paths. Let's explore the relationship between Druidry and these paths, examining the similarities and differences, and how Druidry fits into the broader landscape of modern Paganism.

## Similarities and Shared Philosophies

Druidry shares several core principles with other Pagan paths, which often leads to a harmonious coexistence and cross-pollination of ideas and practices. Some of these shared elements include:

**Nature Reverence:** Like many Pagan paths, Druidry places a strong emphasis on the reverence of nature. This shared belief system fosters a deep connection with the natural world, seeing it as a source of spiritual wisdom and a living entity to be honored and protected.

**Polytheism and Pantheism:** Most Pagan paths, including Druidry, are either polytheistic, worshiping multiple deities, or pantheistic, seeing divinity in all aspects of nature. This allows for a rich tapestry of deities and spiritual beings, often rooted in ancient mythologies and folklore.

**Ritual and Celebration:** Druidry shares with other Pagan paths the practice of marking the cycles of the year through rituals and celebrations. These often align with the solar and lunar cycles, such as solstices, equinoxes, and full moons, and are times for community gathering, reflection, and reverence.

## Distinctions from Other Pagan Paths

While there are many similarities, Druidry also possesses unique aspects that distinguish it from other forms of Paganism:

**Cultural and Historical Roots:** Druidry has its roots in the ancient Celtic cultures of Britain, Ireland, and Western Europe. This specific cultural lineage differentiates it from other Pagan paths that may draw from Norse, Greek, Egyptian, or other ancient traditions.

**The Role of Bards, Ovates, and Druids:** The structured progression through the grades of Bard, Ovate, and Druid is a distinctive feature of many Druidic traditions, emphasizing a journey through different aspects of learning and spiritual growth.

**Emphasis on Art and Creativity:** While all Pagan paths value creativity, Druidry particularly emphasizes the role of the arts in spiritual practice. The Bardic tradition, with its focus on poetry, music, and storytelling, is a central aspect of Druidic practice.

## Interactions and Integration

In the modern context, there is often a fluid interaction between Druidry and other Pagan paths. Practitioners may blend elements from different traditions, creating a personalized spiritual practice that resonates with their beliefs and experiences. This syncretism is often seen as a strength, allowing for a diverse and evolving spiritual practice that can adapt to the needs of contemporary seekers.

For some, Druidry may serve as a primary path, supplemented by practices from other traditions. For others, Druidic practices may be one component of a broader Pagan practice. This flexibility reflects the inclusive and adaptable nature of modern Paganism.

Druidry's place within the broader Pagan landscape is both distinct and integrative. While it maintains its unique identity through its specific cultural roots and practices, it also shares many core principles with other Pagan paths. This relationship allows for a rich exchange of ideas and practices, contributing to the vibrant diversity of modern Pagan spirituality.

In the journey of spiritual exploration, Druidry offers a path that is deeply connected to the ancient Celtic traditions while also being part of the larger tapestry of contemporary Paganism.

## Ancestry and the Modern Druid

In the contemporary practice of Druidry, the concept of ancestry holds a profound significance. So let's explore the role of ancestry in modern Druidry, examining how ancestral heritage and lineage influence and enrich the Druidic path.

## Understanding Ancestry in Druidry

Ancestry in Druidry goes beyond the mere tracing of biological lineage. It encompasses a spiritual connection to those who have come before, both within one's family and the wider historical lineage of Druids and Celtic ancestors.

**Biological Ancestry:** For many modern Druids, exploring their family heritage can be a meaningful journey. It involves understanding where they come from, the cultures and traditions of their ancestors, and how these elements contribute to their identity. This exploration often includes genealogical research and learning about the historical contexts in which their ancestors lived.

**Spiritual Ancestry:** In addition to biological lineage, spiritual ancestry plays a crucial role in Druidry. This concept acknowledges a connection to the ancient Druids and the Celtic ancestors, whose wisdom and traditions form the bedrock of modern practices. Engaging with spiritual ancestry involves studying ancient texts, myths, and practices, and seeking to embody the wisdom of these spiritual forebears.

## Honoring the Ancestors

Honoring the ancestors is a fundamental aspect of Druidic practice. This can be done through various rituals and ceremonies, which serve as a way to remember, honor, and invoke the presence of the ancestors.

**Ancestor Altars:** Many Druids create ancestor altars, which may include photographs, heirlooms, or symbols representing their ancestors. These altars become focal points for remembering and honoring the lineage and can be especially significant during festivals like Samhain, which is traditionally a time for honoring those who have passed.

**Storytelling and Oral Traditions:** Sharing stories about ancestors, whether family stories or ancient myths, is a way to keep their memory alive. This practice not only honors the ancestors but also preserves cultural and family heritage.

## Ancestry and Personal Identity

For modern Druids, exploring ancestry is also a journey of personal identity and growth. Understanding one's roots can provide a sense of belonging and grounding, particularly in a spiritual path that values connection to the past.

**Personal Growth:** Delving into one's ancestry can lead to personal revelations and growth. It may bring to light family patterns, traits, and stories that shape one's identity and life path.

**Cultural Appreciation:** For those whose biological ancestry is not Celtic, engaging with Druidry involves an appreciation and respect for Celtic culture and traditions. This inclusive approach recognizes that one does not need Celtic blood to honor and learn from Celtic wisdom.

In modern Druidry, ancestry is a tapestry woven from threads of biological lineage, spiritual heritage, and cultural learning. It forms an integral part of the Druid's identity, grounding them in a lineage that stretches back through time. By honoring their ancestors, modern Druids create a bridge between the past and the present, ensuring that the wisdom, traditions, and stories of their forebears continue to enrich and inform their spiritual journey.

# CHAPTER 9: SACRED GEOMETRY IN DRUIDIC PRACTICES

In the realm of Druidry, sacred geometry is not merely a collection of shapes but a profound language that speaks of the patterns and principles underlying the natural world. Let's investigate the significance of sacred geometry in Druidic practices, exploring its role in understanding the universe, rituals, and symbolism.

## The Essence of Sacred Geometry

Sacred geometry is the study of geometric shapes and proportions that are considered sacred, reflecting the patterns of creation and the fundamental structures of the universe. In Druidry, it is seen as a key to unlocking the mysteries of nature's designs, from the spirals of galaxies to the symmetry of flowers.

**Patterns of Creation:** Sacred geometry is observed in the natural world, where its principles manifest in the arrangement of leaves, the structure of crystals, and the patterns of animal markings. Druids believe these patterns are a reflection of the divine blueprint of creation.

**Cosmic Harmony:** Sacred geometry is also seen as a representation of the harmonious relationships between all things. It reflects the interconnectedness of the universe and the cycles of growth, decay, and rebirth.

## Sacred Geometry in Rituals and Symbolism

In Druidic rituals and symbolism, sacred geometry is used to align with the energies of the natural world and the cosmos.

**Creating Sacred Spaces:** When Druids create sacred spaces, such as groves or altars, they often use principles of sacred geometry. The circle, a fundamental shape, represents wholeness and infinity. Aligning ritual spaces with the cardinal points and celestial bodies, Druids reflect the geometric order of the heavens.

**Symbols and Tools:** Many Druidic symbols incorporate aspects of sacred geometry. For instance, the Awen symbol, with its three rays, represents balance and the flow of energy. The use of wands and staffs can also be seen as aligning with the line, a basic component of geometry, symbolizing direction and connection between two points.

## Sacred Geometry in Personal Practice

For the modern Druid, integrating sacred geometry into personal practice can enhance their connection to the natural world and the spiritual realm.

**Meditation and Visualization:** Meditating on geometric shapes can be a way to tap into deeper levels of consciousness and the universal patterns they represent. Visualization of shapes like spirals, circles, and triangles can aid in focusing energy and intention.

**Learning from Nature:** By observing and studying the geometry present in nature, Druids can gain insights into the workings of the natural world and how to live in harmony with it. This practice can be as simple as observing the patterns in leaves or the arrangement of petals in a flower.

Sacred geometry is a key element in the tapestry of Druidic practice, offering a way to understand and align with the fundamental patterns of the universe. Whether through ritual, symbolism, or personal study, engaging with sacred geometry allows Druids to deepen their connection to the natural world and the intricate patterns that weave through all of existence. In this way, sacred geometry serves as both a tool for spiritual growth and a reminder of the beautiful complexity of the cosmos.

## The Esoteric Traditions of Druidry

Let's investigate the esoteric traditions of Druidry, a facet that often remains shrouded in mystery. These traditions encompass the deeper, more mystical aspects of Druidic practice, offering insight into the spiritual and metaphysical dimensions of this ancient path.

## The Veil of Mystery in Druidic Esotericism

Esoteric Druidry refers to the aspects of Druidic practice that are typically hidden or reserved for the more dedicated practitioner. These elements often require deeper study and a more profound understanding of the Druidic path.

**Historical Context:** The esoteric aspects of Druidry have their roots in the ancient Druidic traditions, where knowledge was passed down orally and reserved for initiates. This secrecy was partly due to the sacredness of the knowledge and partly as a response to historical challenges, particularly during times when Druidic practices were suppressed.

**Modern Interpretations:** In contemporary Druidry, esoteric traditions are often interpreted through a modern lens. This involves a blend of historical understanding, personal insight, and adaptation to current contexts, making the esoteric traditions both dynamic and evolving.

## Core Esoteric Practices

Esoteric Druidry encompasses a range of practices that aim to deepen the spiritual journey and connect with the divine.

**Meditation and Visualization:** These practices are central to esoteric Druidry, used as tools for inner journeying, connecting with the divine, and accessing deeper wisdom. Visualization techniques often involve journeying to the Otherworld, a realm in Druidic cosmology that is home to deities, ancestors, and spirit guides.

**Divination and Prophecy:** Druids historically were known for their skills in divination and prophecy. Modern esoteric practices include the use of Ogham staves, tarot cards, or scrying to gain insights into the past, present, and future.

## The Mystical Path of Druidry

Esoteric Druidry is deeply intertwined with the mystical pursuit of understanding the nature of reality and one's place within it.

**Connection with the Natural World: At** its core, esoteric Druidry maintains a profound connection with the natural world. This connection is not just physical but deeply spiritual, viewing nature as a manifestation of the divine.

**The Quest for Inner Knowledge:** Esoteric Druidry places great emphasis on the inner journey, seeking knowledge and enlightenment. This path involves exploring the depths of one's consciousness and understanding the subtle energies that govern the universe.

The esoteric traditions of Druidry offer a pathway to deeper spiritual understanding and a more profound connection with the natural and divine realms. These practices, while often shrouded in mystery, provide a rich and nuanced perspective on the Druidic path, inviting practitioners to explore the depths of their spirituality and the mysteries of the universe. Through meditation, divination, and a deep connection with nature, esoteric Druidry continues to be a vital and evolving aspect of the modern Druidic practice.

# CHAPTER 10: DRUIDIC HERBALISM

Let's explore the green heart of Druidry and the intermediate aspects of Druidic herbalism and uncover the rich tradition of plant knowledge and its applications in modern Druidic practices, blending ancient lore with contemporary understanding.

## The Roots of Druidic Herbalism

Druidic herbalism is deeply entwined with the Druidic reverence for nature. It encompasses a holistic approach to plants, viewing them not just as physical entities but as spiritual beings with their own energies and spirits.

**Historical Perspectives:** The ancient Druids were renowned for their extensive knowledge of plants and their properties. They used this knowledge for healing, rituals, and creating sacred spaces. Although much of the specific plant lore has been lost over time, contemporary Druids draw on historical texts, folklore, and intuitive practices to reconnect with this tradition.

**Modern Adaptations:** In the modern context, Druidic herbalism often intersects with other herbal traditions. It emphasizes a sustainable and respectful approach to plant use, focusing on local flora and the ethical harvesting of plants. This practice is not just about using herbs for physical healing but also for spiritual and energetic purposes.

## Druidic Herbal Practices

Druidic herbalism is as much an art as it is a science, involving both practical knowledge and intuitive understanding.

**Medicinal and Ritual Use:** Herbs in Druidry are used for healing the body, mind, and spirit. This includes creating herbal remedies, teas, and tinctures for physical ailments, as well as using herbs in rituals and ceremonies for spiritual healing and protection. The choice of herbs is often guided by both their medicinal properties and their symbolic meanings within Druidic lore.

**Connecting with Plant Spirits:** An essential aspect of Druidic herbalism is developing a relationship with the spirit of the plants. This involves understanding the essence and energy of each herb, and how it can be used in harmony with the practitioner's intentions. Meditation, communication, and offering gratitude to the plants are key practices in this process.

**Herbal Magic and Divination:** Druidic herbalism also extends to magical practices, where herbs are used in spellwork, amulets, and divination. The properties of herbs are harnessed to amplify intentions, protect, or attract certain energies. This practice requires a deep understanding of the symbolic and energetic properties of different plants.

## Herbal Wisdom in Druidry

This section delves deeper into the wisdom and knowledge embedded in Druidic herbalism, highlighting its significance in the broader context of Druidic practices.

**The Wheel of the Year and Herbalism:** The use of herbs is closely tied to the Druidic Wheel of the Year. Certain herbs are associated with specific festivals and seasons, reflecting their natural cycles and the energies of the time. For instance, mistletoe is particularly revered during the Winter Solstice, while Beltane might focus on the vitality of spring herbs.

**Educational and Preservation Efforts:** Modern Druids are often involved in educational initiatives to share knowledge about herbs and their uses. This includes workshops, written resources, and community gardens. There is also a focus on the conservation of plant species and the preservation of natural habitats, reflecting the Druidic commitment to ecological stewardship.

**Integrating Herbalism into Daily Life:** Practical advice on integrating Druidic herbalism into daily life includes creating a personal herb garden, ethically foraging for wild herbs, and incorporating herbal practices in daily rituals and self-care routines.

Druidic Herbalism presents a pathway to connect deeply with the natural world, tapping into the ancient wisdom of plants for healing, spiritual growth, and ecological harmony. It's a practice that encourages respect for nature, self-awareness, and a sustainable lifestyle, resonating with the core values of modern Druidry.

## Celestial Bodies and Druidic Cosmology

Let's investigate the fascinating interplay between Druidry and celestial bodies, exploring how the movements and energies of the moon, stars, and other celestial phenomena are integral to Druidic belief systems and practices. We can bridge ancient wisdom with contemporary understandings of the cosmos, providing a comprehensive guide to celestial Druidry.

## Understanding Celestial Influence in Druidry

The celestial bodies have always held a profound significance in Druidic cosmology. They are not only seen as physical entities but also as spiritual symbols and guides.

**The Moon's Phases and Druidry:** The lunar cycle plays a crucial role in Druidic practices. Each phase of the moon, from the new moon to the full moon, symbolizes different energies and aspects of life. For instance, the new moon is often associated with new beginnings and the full moon with culmination and clarity. Druidic rituals and ceremonies are often aligned with these lunar phases to maximize their spiritual potency.

**The Stars and Constellations:** Druids have traditionally paid close attention to the stars and constellations, using them for navigation, divination, and as a calendar. The positioning of certain stars and constellations at different times of the year signals the shifting of seasons and is often used to time festivals and rituals. The study of celestial patterns also offers insights into the deeper workings of the universe from a Druidic perspective.

**Solar Cycles and Druidic Festivals:** The sun's journey across the sky and the changing seasons are closely observed and celebrated in Druidry. Festivals such as the solstices and equinoxes mark key points in the solar cycle, each bearing its own spiritual significance and rituals. These festivals help Druids attune to the natural rhythm of the earth and the sun, fostering a deeper connection with the natural world.

## Celestial Symbolism and Mythology

Druidic cosmology is rich in symbolism and mythology related to celestial bodies, offering a metaphysical understanding of the universe.

**Mythological Representations:** Many Celtic myths and legends involve celestial themes, with gods and goddesses often embodying astronomical phenomena. For example, the moon goddesses in Celtic mythology are associated with intuition, wisdom, and the feminine divine, reflecting the moon's influence in Druidic spirituality.

**Astrological Interpretations:** While not astrology in the conventional sense, Druids often interpret celestial patterns and alignments as omens or messages from the divine. This involves a more intuitive and symbolic approach, focusing on the spiritual and energetic implications of celestial events.

**The Cosmic Dance:** Druids view the movements of celestial bodies as part of a cosmic dance or cycle, which reflects the interconnectedness of all things. This perspective encourages a holistic understanding of one's place in the universe, emphasizing harmony with the celestial rhythms.

## Practical Applications in Modern Druidry

Incorporating celestial elements into modern Druidic practice can be both meaningful and enriching.

**Observation and Meditation:** Regular observation of the moon, stars, and sun fosters a deeper appreciation of the celestial cycles. Combined with meditation, this practice can lead to profound spiritual insights and a sense of cosmic connectedness.

**Rituals and Ceremonies:** Celestial phenomena can be integrated into Druidic rituals and ceremonies. This might include moon rituals, star gazing sessions, and celebrations of solar festivals, each designed to align with and draw upon the energies of these celestial bodies.

**Learning and Teaching:** For those interested in deepening their understanding, studying celestial phenomena from a Druidic perspective can be a rewarding pursuit. Sharing this knowledge through teaching and community gatherings helps keep the tradition alive and evolving.

Celestial bodies play a significant role in Druidic cosmology and practice. By understanding and aligning with these celestial patterns, modern Druids can deepen their spiritual practice and connection to the universe, continuing a tradition that has been a pillar of Druidry since ancient times.

# CHAPTER 11: THE ENERGETICS OF STONE CIRCLES

It's time to explore the spiritual and energetic significance of ancient stone circles within Druidic practices. These ancient structures, often shrouded in mystery, have been central to various spiritual traditions, including Druidry. Their significance lies not just in their historical and archaeological value but also in their profound energetic and symbolic meanings.

## Understanding Stone Circles in Druidic Context

Stone circles have been a source of fascination and reverence throughout history. In Druidry, they are seen as more than just arrangements of rocks; they are viewed as sacred spaces where the boundaries between the physical and spiritual worlds become thin.

**Historical Significance:** Many stone circles date back to the Neolithic and Bronze Age periods. Their precise purpose remains largely unknown, but they are thought to have been used for astronomical observations, rituals, and as places of gathering for ancient communities. In Druidry, these sites are respected as connections to ancestors and ancient wisdom.

**Energetic Hotspots:** It is believed that stone circles were intentionally built at places where the Earth's energy is particularly strong. These sites are often located at ley lines or Earth's energy lines, making them powerful spots for spiritual practices. Druids harness these energies in their rituals, meditation, and healing work.

**Symbolic Representations:** Each stone circle has its unique configuration and energy, which can symbolize various aspects of life, death, and rebirth. The circular layout represents the cycle of life, continuity, and connection to the universe. They serve as reminders of the interconnectedness of all things.

## Experiencing Stone Circles in Modern Druidry

Incorporating stone circles into modern Druidic practice offers a unique way to connect with the Earth's energy and ancient traditions.

**Visiting and Connecting with Stone Circles:** Visiting these ancient sites can be a profound experience. Druids often perform rituals, meditate, or simply sit in silence within these circles, feeling the energy and listening to the whispers of ancient times. It is an opportunity to connect with the ancestors and the natural world in a deeply spiritual way.

**Rituals and Ceremonies:** Many modern Druids use stone circles for seasonal ceremonies, particularly during solstices and equinoxes. These ancient sites provide a powerful backdrop for rituals that honor the natural cycles of the Earth and the cosmos.

**Personal and Collective Healing:** The energetic properties of stone circles are believed to facilitate healing. Druids may use these sites to perform healing rituals or to meditate for personal and collective healing, tapping into the Earth's energy for restoration and balance.

## The Role of Stone Circles in Eco-Spirituality

The reverence for stone circles in Druidry also highlights a deep ecological understanding and respect for the Earth.

**Sacred Geography:** Understanding the sacredness of the land and its features, like stone circles, encourages a respectful and sustainable relationship with the Earth. It fosters an eco-spiritual awareness, recognizing the Earth as a living, sacred being.

**Preservation and Protection:** Druidic interest in stone circles goes hand in hand with efforts to preserve these ancient sites. Modern Druids often advocate for the protection and respectful treatment of these and other sacred sites, emphasizing the importance of heritage and the Earth's sanctity.

**Connecting with the Land:** Engaging with stone circles is a way to deepen one's connection with the land and its history. It provides a tangible link to the past and a reminder of humanity's enduring relationship with nature.

Stone circles play a significant role in the Druidic tradition, serving as portals to the past, energetic hotspots, and symbols of life's cyclical nature. They are a testament to the ancient wisdom that continues to inspire and guide modern Druidry, embedding a deep sense of respect and reverence for the natural world and its mysterious history.

## Runes and Ogham: Written Mysteries

Let's delve into the mystical realms of runes and Ogham within the context of Druidry, offering a more advanced look at these ancient systems of writing and their magical applications. These symbolic scripts are not just tools of communication but are imbued with deep spiritual meanings and are integral to the practice of Druidic magic and divination.

## The Mystique of Runes in Druidic Practice

**Origins and Evolution:** Originating from the ancient Germanic tribes, runes are an alphabet where each character holds specific meanings and energies. Over the centuries, their use has evolved from mundane writing to powerful symbols in divination and spellwork. Although not originally part of the Celtic Druid tradition, they have been adopted and adapted due to their profound spiritual resonance.

**Runes as Magical Symbols:** In Druidry, each rune is believed to encapsulate the essence of the forces it represents, from natural elements to abstract concepts. They are used in magical work for their power to influence and manifest change. For instance, the rune *Fehu*, representing wealth, might be used in rituals to attract abundance.

**Divinatory Practices:** Runes are also powerful tools for divination. Casting runes allows a Druid to gain insights into the present and potential futures, guiding them to understand the path ahead. This practice involves not only interpretation based on the symbolism of the runes but also an intuitive understanding of their deeper messages.

## Exploring Ogham: The Druidic Tree Alphabet

**Ogham's Celtic Roots:** Unlike runes, Ogham is a script that originated within Celtic society and is closely associated with Druidic traditions. Known as the tree alphabet, each character corresponds to a specific tree or plant, reflecting the Druids' deep reverence for nature.

**Ogham in Ritual and Divination:** Ogham staves, made of wood or stone, are used in divinatory practices. Each stave's connection to a particular tree or plant imbues it with unique energies and meanings. For example, the *Birch* stave, known as *Beith* in Ogham, is often associated with new beginnings and purification.

**A Tool for Meditation and Magic:** Beyond divination, Ogham is used in meditation and magical workings. Contemplating a specific Ogham stave can help a Druid connect with the attributes of the corresponding tree, fostering a deeper bond with the natural world and enhancing their spiritual and magical practices.

## Integrating Runes and Ogham into Modern Druidry

**Personalized Practices:** Modern Druids often develop their unique relationship with runes and Ogham. Some might use them in combination, while others may prefer to specialize in one. Their use is highly personal and reflective of each Druid's path and connection with these ancient scripts.

**Educational and Spiritual Journey:** Learning and working with runes and Ogham is a journey of both education and spiritual exploration. It involves studying the historical and cultural backgrounds of these scripts, as well as developing an intuitive understanding of their deeper meanings.

**Creating Sacred Space:** Many Druids create sacred spaces with runes and Ogham, using them to mark the boundaries of ritual circles or to adorn altars. This not only adds a layer of magical protection but also enhances the spiritual potency of the ritual space.

We have uncovered the rich and mystical world of runes and Ogham in Druidry, offering insights into their historical backgrounds, spiritual meanings, and practical applications. These ancient scripts are more than mere alphabets; they are keys to unlocking deeper magical and spiritual knowledge, serving as vital tools for divination, meditation, and magical workings in the modern Druidic path.

# CHAPTER 12: ANIMAL TOTEMS AND SPIRIT GUIDES

Now we turn to the mystical connection between Druidry and the animal kingdom, focusing on the significance of animal totems and spirit guides as we explore the deep symbiotic relationship between Druids and various animal energies, unraveling the spiritual and symbolic meanings of these connections.

### Understanding Animal Totems in Druidic Tradition

**The Concept of Animal Totems:** In Druidry, an animal totem is not just a symbol but a spiritual entity that represents certain qualities, strengths, and insights. These totems are believed to guide, protect, and communicate wisdom to the practitioner. They are more than mere symbols or metaphors; they are revered as spiritual allies.

**Identifying Personal Totems:** Discovering one's animal totem is a journey of self-exploration and spiritual awakening. It often involves meditation, observation, and reflection. The process is highly personal and intuitive, with many Druids believing that a totem chooses the individual, revealing itself in dreams, visions, or through recurring encounters in the natural world.

**Working with Animal Totems:** Once identified, Druids work with their animal totems in various ways. This can include invoking the totem in rituals, meditating on its qualities, or seeking guidance from it during challenging times. Each totem brings unique insights and strengths, aiding the Druid in their spiritual journey and everyday life.

## The Role of Spirit Guides

**Spirit Guides in Druidic Practices:** Spirit guides in Druidry are often perceived as manifestations of animal spirits but can also encompass ancestors, mythical beings, or even elemental forces. They serve as intermediaries between the physical and spiritual worlds, offering guidance, protection, and wisdom.

**Communicating with Spirit Guides:** Interaction with spirit guides is a key component of Druidic practice. It often occurs during meditative states, rituals, or through divination practices. The communication is not always verbal; it can be symbolic or through intuitive understanding.

**Spirit Guides and Personal Growth:** Engaging with spirit guides can be transformative. They often challenge individuals to grow, heal, and understand deeper truths about themselves and the world around them. This relationship is dynamic and evolves as the Druid progresses on their spiritual path.

## Integrating Animal Energies into Druidic Practices

**Rituals and Ceremonies:** Animals and their symbolic meanings play a crucial role in Druidic rituals and ceremonies. For instance, a Druid may call upon the energy of a hawk for clarity of vision during a ritual, or a bear for strength and protection.

**Ecological Connection and Respect:** The Druidic path emphasizes a harmonious relationship with nature. Working with animal totems and spirit guides reinforces this connection, fostering a deeper respect for the natural world and its inhabitants.

**Personal and Collective Insights:** Animal totems and spirit guides provide not just personal insights but also collective wisdom. They are seen as links to the ancestral past and the collective unconscious, offering guidance that transcends individual experiences.

## Elemental Forces and the Four Directions

The mystical world of elemental forces and the four cardinal directions are central to many Druidic rituals and practices. Let's explore how these elemental forces and directions are understood, respected, and integrated into Druidic life and spirituality.

### Understanding the Elemental Forces

**The Quintessence of Elements:** In Druidry, the elements – Earth, Air, Fire, Water, and Spirit – are seen as fundamental forces of nature and the universe. Each element represents specific aspects of life and the natural world, playing a vital role in maintaining balance and harmony.

**Earth - Stability and Grounding:** Earth symbolizes stability, grounding, and fertility. It is associated with the physical world, nature, and the body. In rituals, invoking the Earth element is about connecting with the physical realm and seeking grounding and stability.

**Air - Intellect and Communication:** Air represents intellect, communication, and knowledge. It is linked to the mental realm, thoughts, and wisdom. Druidic practices involving Air focus on the pursuit of knowledge, clarity of thought, and effective communication.

**Fire - Transformation and Energy:** Fire symbolizes transformation, energy, and passion. It is associated with change, inspiration, and courage. Rituals invoking Fire often seek to harness its transformative power for personal growth and spiritual awakening.

**Water - Emotion and Intuition:** Water represents emotion, intuition, and the subconscious. It is linked to feelings, dreams, and psychic abilities. In Druidic practices, Water is invoked for emotional healing, enhancing intuition, and exploring the subconscious.

**Spirit - The Unifying Force:** Spirit, often seen as the fifth element, represents the unifying force of the universe, connecting all things. It is associated with the divine, the soul, and the unseen energies that permeate all existence.

## The Four Directions and Druidic Rituals

**Significance of the Four Directions:** The four cardinal directions – North, East, South, and West – are integral to Druidic rituals. Each direction is aligned with specific elements and energies, offering unique attributes and powers to rituals and ceremonies.

**Aligning with the Directions:** Druidic practices often involve aligning with the four directions during rituals to harness their energies. This alignment is both a physical act, such as facing a specific direction, and a spiritual one, involving meditation and invocation.

**Creating Sacred Space:** In Druidry, casting a circle or creating sacred space often involves calling upon the four directions. This act acknowledges and invites the energies of each direction, creating a balanced and protected space for rituals and spiritual work.

## Integrating Elemental and Directional Energies

**Personal and Ecological Balance:** Working with elements and directions is not only about personal spiritual practice but also about recognizing and maintaining ecological balance. Druids see themselves as part of the natural world, and these practices reinforce their connection to the Earth and its cycles.

**Rituals and Daily Practices:** Elemental and directional energies are incorporated into various Druidic rituals, from seasonal celebrations to rites of passage. In daily practices, Druids might meditate on a specific element or direction to bring balance to an aspect of their life.

**Healing and Divination:** Elements and directions are also used in Druidic healing practices and divination. For example, a Druid might use stones or crystals representing different elements for healing purposes or use the directions as a guide in divinatory readings.

It is important to encourage a deeper understanding and respect for these primal energies, inviting Druids to harmonize with the natural world and its elemental powers.

# CHAPTER 13: ADVANCED RITUAL TECHNIQUES

As we delve into the deeper aspects of Druidic practice, we look to provide an in-depth understanding of the sophisticated rituals that form the backbone of advanced Druidic practice. These rituals, evolved and refined over centuries, are not just mere ceremonies but are considered powerful tools for transformation, connection with the natural world, and spiritual enlightenment.

## The Evolution of Ritual in Druidry

To appreciate the complexity and depth of advanced Druidic rituals, it's essential to understand their evolution. Initially, Druidic rituals were simple, focusing on the cycles of nature and the basic elements of earth, air, fire, and water. As Druidry evolved, these rituals became more elaborate, integrating aspects of celestial movements, sacred geometry, and deep esoteric knowledge.

This evolution reflects a growing understanding of the universe and the Druid's place within it. The rituals thus transformed from straightforward seasonal celebrations to intricate ceremonies that involve detailed preparations, specific invocations, and the use of complex symbols and tools.

## Components of Advanced Rituals

Advanced Druidic rituals are multifaceted and can vary significantly in their composition and purpose. However, certain elements are commonly found in these practices:

**Preparation and Purification:** Preparation is crucial in advanced rituals. This can involve fasting, meditation, and purification practices such as bathing in natural waters or using sacred herbs like sage for smudging. The purification of the ritual space is also essential, often done with elements like water and fire to cleanse and consecrate the area.

**Sacred Geometry and Alignment:** Many advanced rituals incorporate the principles of sacred geometry, aligning the ritual space with specific patterns like the Flower of Life or the Celtic Spiral. These patterns are believed to resonate with cosmic energies and help align the participants with the natural order of the universe.

**Celestial Timing:** The alignment of rituals with celestial events - such as solstices, equinoxes, lunar phases, and specific astrological configurations - is a common practice. These timings are chosen for their powerful energetic influences and their symbolic meanings.

**Invocation and Chanting:** Advanced rituals often involve the invocation of deities, ancestral spirits, or natural forces. This is typically done through chanting, singing, or reciting specific verses or mantras that are believed to have vibrational powers.

**Use of Advanced Tools:** While basic tools like wands and staffs are common in Druidry, advanced rituals may include more specialized items. These can range from intricately carved stones and crystals to specially crafted ritual garments and uniquely designed altars.

## The Purpose and Power of Advanced Rituals

Advanced rituals in Druidry are not merely ceremonial but serve multiple purposes:

**Transformation and Healing:** Many advanced rituals are designed for personal transformation and healing, aiding participants in their spiritual journey and personal growth.

**Connection with the Divine:** These rituals often aim to establish a profound connection with the divine forces of nature, the ancestors, or the Celtic pantheon of gods and goddesses.

**Eco-Spiritual Work:** Reflecting Druidry's deep connection with nature, some advanced rituals focus on healing the Earth, aligning with its energy lines, and working towards ecological balance.

Advanced ritual techniques in Druidry are a testament to the tradition's depth and its continuous evolution. These practices, steeped in ancient wisdom and adapted to modern understanding, offer a pathway to profound spiritual experiences. They serve not only as a bridge to the past but also as a relevant and powerful tool for personal and collective transformation in the contemporary world.

In embracing these advanced rituals, modern Druids continue a rich legacy, adapting and evolving the ancient ways to find harmony and wisdom in the complexities of the modern era.

## Druidry and the Modern World

Druidry, with its deep roots in ancient Celtic traditions, has seen a significant resurgence in the modern era. So let's explore the ways in which Druidry interacts with, influences, and is influenced by contemporary societal and environmental issues. The focus is on three main areas: the role of Druidry in environmental activism, its integration with modern lifestyles, and the challenges and opportunities faced by Druids in today's world.

## Druidry as a Force for Environmental Advocacy

One of the most prominent aspects of modern Druidry is its strong emphasis on environmental protection and activism. Druids, with their deep reverence for nature and belief in the sacredness of the Earth, are often found at the forefront of ecological movements. They bring a unique spiritual perspective to environmental issues, viewing the protection of the natural world not just as a practical necessity but as a sacred duty. This belief system aligns closely with many contemporary concerns about climate change, biodiversity loss, and environmental degradation.

Druidic practices, rituals, and teachings often emphasize the interconnectedness of all life, a concept that resonates powerfully in the context of ecological sustainability. Modern Druids use their gatherings, such as those during the Wheel of the Year festivals, to raise awareness about environmental issues and to foster a sense of community around shared ecological values. They also engage in practical actions, from tree planting and conservation efforts to participating in environmental protests and policy advocacy.

## Integrating Druidry with Contemporary Lifestyles

Another aspect of Druidry's modern resurgence is its adaptability to contemporary lifestyles. In a world dominated by technology and rapid change, Druidry offers a way to reconnect with nature and find balance. Modern Druids come from all walks of life and incorporate their beliefs and practices into their daily routines in various ways. This can range from simple mindfulness practices and nature walks to elaborate rituals and celebrations.

The challenge for many modern Druids is finding ways to practice their faith authentically within the constraints of a busy, technology-driven world. Some have turned to online communities and digital platforms to share knowledge, connect with other Druids, and organize events. Others focus on integrating Druidic principles into their professional lives, advocating for sustainable practices and ethical decision-making in their workplaces.

## Challenges and Opportunities in the 21st Century

As Druidry continues to evolve, it faces both challenges and opportunities. One significant challenge is the risk of commercialization and dilution of Druidic practices. As interest in spirituality and nature-based religions grows, there is a danger that the core principles and traditions of Druidry could be co-opted or misrepresented. This requires a careful balance between preserving ancient traditions and adapting to contemporary contexts.

On the other hand, the modern era presents unique opportunities for Druidry. The global environmental crisis has led to a widespread reawakening of interest in earth-centered spirituality. Druidry's message of reverence for nature and ecological responsibility resonates strongly with many people seeking a more sustainable and balanced way of life. Additionally, the increasing interconnectedness of the world provides opportunities for Druidic communities to network and collaborate on a global scale, spreading their message and influencing larger societal and environmental changes.

The resurgence of Druidry in the modern world is a testament to its enduring relevance and adaptability. As a spiritual path deeply rooted in the reverence for nature, Druidry offers valuable perspectives and practices for addressing some of the most pressing challenges of our time. Its integration into contemporary lifestyles and its role in environmental advocacy highlight the dynamic and evolving nature of this ancient path.

# CHAPTER 14: ECO-SPIRITUALITY AND DRUIDIC PRACTICES

In the tapestry of modern Druidry, eco-spirituality stands out as a vibrant thread, intertwining the ancient wisdom of Druidic practices with contemporary environmental consciousness. Let's explore the essence of eco-spirituality within Druidry, its manifestation in modern practices, and the broader implications for our relationship with the natural world.

## The Essence of Eco-Spirituality in Druidry

Eco-spirituality in Druidry is rooted in the profound reverence for the Earth and all its inhabitants. This perspective sees the natural world not as a resource to be exploited but as a sacred, living entity deserving respect and protection. The Druidic belief in the interconnectedness of all life forms the foundation of eco-spirituality, emphasizing that human well-being is intrinsically linked to the health of the Earth.

Modern Druids express this connection through various practices that honor the Earth, such as seasonal celebrations that align with the cycles of nature, rituals that invoke the spirits of land, sea, and sky, and meditations that foster a deep sense of oneness with the natural world. These practices are not only spiritual expressions but also serve to remind practitioners of their duty to protect and preserve the environment.

## Eco-Spirituality in Practice

In practical terms, eco-spirituality in Druidry manifests in several ways. Many Druids engage in environmental activism, advocating for policies and actions that safeguard the natural world. This activism can take the form of participating in protests, supporting conservation efforts, and promoting sustainable living.

Another important aspect is the use of natural spaces for spiritual practices. Sacred groves, stone circles, and bodies of water are often the settings for Druidic rituals and gatherings, highlighting the significance of these natural sites. The protection and maintenance of these spaces become a form of spiritual stewardship for many Druids.

Furthermore, eco-spirituality is reflected in the everyday choices and lifestyles of modern Druids. This might include adopting a more sustainable lifestyle, engaging in practices like permaculture or organic gardening, and making conscious choices to reduce one's environmental footprint.

## Broader Implications for Humanity and Nature

The eco-spiritual approach of Druidry offers broader lessons for humanity's relationship with nature. It challenges the dominant paradigm of viewing nature as merely a resource and advocates for a more harmonious, respectful relationship with the Earth. This shift in perspective is crucial in addressing the environmental crises facing the planet, such as climate change, biodiversity loss, and pollution.

By integrating ancient wisdom with modern environmental ethics, Druidry's eco-spirituality provides a powerful framework for rethinking how we interact with our environment. It encourages a move away from exploitative practices towards a more sustainable, balanced way of living that honors the Earth as a sacred, living system.

The integration of eco-spirituality into modern Druidic practices represents a vital and transformative aspect of this ancient spiritual path. It not only enriches the spiritual lives of its practitioners but also contributes to the broader movement towards a more sustainable and harmonious relationship with the natural world. Through its teachings and practices, Druidry offers valuable insights and tools for fostering a deeper connection with the Earth and advocating for its protection and preservation.

## The Druid in the Digital Age

In the evolving landscape of the 21st century, the ancient path of Druidry finds itself intersecting with the digital age. Let's explore how technology influences and shapes modern Druidic practice, from the way Druids connect and learn to the integration of digital tools in spiritual practices.

## Digital Connectivity and Community Building

One of the most significant impacts of technology on modern Druidry is in the realm of community building and connectivity. With the advent of the internet and social media, Druids from around the world can connect, share knowledge, and participate in discussions regardless of geographical boundaries. Online forums, social media groups, and websites dedicated to Druidry have become vibrant hubs of activity where practitioners can exchange ideas, find support, and deepen their understanding of Druidic principles.

These digital platforms have also enabled the creation of virtual gatherings, rituals, and celebrations. Especially in times when physical gatherings are not possible, these online spaces provide an invaluable means for maintaining community connections and continuing spiritual practices. They offer a way for those who may be isolated due to location or other circumstances to participate in the Druidic community.

## Technology in Spiritual Practice

The integration of technology into spiritual practice is another area where the digital age intersects with Druidry. While the core of Druidic practice remains rooted in nature and personal experience, technology can enhance these experiences in various ways. For instance, mobile apps for meditation, guided imagery, and nature sounds can aid in creating a conducive environment for spiritual practices, especially for those living in urban areas.

Additionally, technology has made a wealth of resources readily available for those seeking to learn about Druidry. E-books, online courses, podcasts, and video tutorials have made it easier than ever to access information about Druidic history, philosophy, and practices. This democratization of knowledge has played a significant role in the resurgence and spread of Druidry in the modern world.

## Balancing Technology and Tradition

Despite the benefits, the integration of technology into Druidic practice is not without its challenges. One of the key concerns is maintaining a balance between embracing useful technological tools and preserving the essential nature-based and experiential aspects of Druidry. There is a delicate balance to be struck between using technology as a tool to enhance practice and allowing it to overshadow the fundamental principles of connection with nature, personal introspection, and experiential learning.

Druids in the digital age are tasked with navigating this balance, finding ways to use technology that support and enhance their practice without detracting from the core values of Druidry. This may involve setting boundaries around technology use, consciously choosing when and how to engage with digital tools, and always prioritizing direct experience and connection with the natural world.

The intersection of Druidry and the digital age offers both opportunities and challenges. Technology has played a crucial role in the spread and evolution of modern Druidry, offering new ways to connect, learn, and practice. However, maintaining the essence of Druidry in an increasingly digital world requires a conscious effort to balance the use of technology with the traditional, nature-centered focus of the path. As Druidry continues to evolve, this balance will be key to preserving its integrity and relevance in the modern world.

# CHAPTER 15: ADVANCED DIVINATION METHODS IN MODERN DRUIDRY

Divination, the practice of seeking knowledge of the future or the unknown by supernatural means, has been a cornerstone of Druidic practices since ancient times. In modern Druidry, advanced divination methods have evolved, integrating traditional techniques with contemporary insights. Let's explore these advanced methods, their significance, and their application in the modern Druidic path.

## The Evolution of Druidic Divination

Historically, Druids were known for their skill in divination, which was used for guidance, decision-making, and understanding the will of the divine. Ancient methods included augury (interpreting the flight patterns of birds), omens, and the casting of lots using objects like stones or bones. Over time, these practices have evolved, incorporating elements from various cultural and spiritual traditions.

In modern Druidry, divination is not seen as mere fortune-telling but as a deep and meaningful practice that connects the practitioner with the natural world and the deeper currents of life.

It involves interpreting signs and symbols not just to predict the future, but to gain insight into the present and to understand the interplay of various forces and energies at work.

## Contemporary Techniques in Druidic Divination

Modern Druids employ a variety of advanced divination methods, each with its unique symbolism and methodology. Some of the most prominent techniques include:

**Ogham Divination**: Ogham is an ancient alphabet, where each character is associated with a specific tree or plant. Modern Druids use Ogham for divination by carving or drawing these characters on pieces of wood or stone, casting them, and interpreting their arrangement and orientation.

**Geomancy**: This method involves interpreting patterns formed by tossed handfuls of soil, rocks, or sand. In a contemporary setting, this can also be done using specially marked dice or randomly generated dots on paper.

**Tarot and Oracle Cards**: While not originally part of ancient Druidic practices, many modern Druids use Tarot and oracle cards, often with imagery and themes resonant with Celtic mythology and Druidic symbolism.

**Astrology**: Celtic astrology, based on lunar cycles and the Celtic Tree Calendar, is another tool for divination. It involves interpreting the positions of celestial bodies to provide guidance and insights.

**Nature-Based Divination**: This includes observing natural phenomena such as weather patterns, animal behavior, and the growth patterns of plants. Modern Druids often see these as messages from the natural world or the divine.

## Application and Interpretation in Modern Contexts

The application of these divination methods in modern Druidry extends beyond personal guidance. It is also used in community decision-making, spiritual development, and understanding ecological and social patterns.

The interpretation of divinatory signs in Druidry is a skill that requires intuition, knowledge, and a deep connection with the spiritual and natural worlds. Modern Druids often spend years honing their skills in divination, learning to understand the complex interplay of symbolism, intuition, and observation.

Moreover, divination in Druidry is approached with a sense of responsibility. It is understood that the insights gained are not deterministic but offer potential pathways and perspectives. The emphasis is on empowering the individual or community to make informed choices rather than prescribing a fixed course of action.

Advanced divination methods in modern Druidry represent a rich and complex blend of ancient traditions and contemporary insights. These practices provide a means for Druids to engage deeply with the spiritual and natural worlds, offering guidance, wisdom, and a deeper understanding of the intricate tapestry of life. As a part of the modern Druidic path, they embody a living tradition that evolves and adapts to the needs and understandings of each generation.

## Sacred Journeys: Pilgrimages and Quests in Modern Druidry

The concept of a sacred journey, a pilgrimage or quest, holds a special place in the Druidic tradition. These spiritual journeys, whether physical or metaphorical, are central to the Druidic pursuit of wisdom, connection with the natural world, and personal transformation. In modern Druidry, these journeys have adapted to contemporary contexts while retaining their profound spiritual significance.

## The Nature of Sacred Journeys in Druidry

Sacred journeys in Druidry can take various forms, ranging from physical pilgrimages to specific natural or historical sites, to inner quests for knowledge and spiritual growth. These journeys are seen as opportunities for deepening one's connection with the Earth, the ancestors, and the divine. They are times of reflection, learning, and significant life transitions.

**Physical Pilgrimages**: These involve traveling to places of historical or spiritual significance to the Druid path. Sites like ancient stone circles, sacred groves, and wells are common pilgrimage destinations. Modern Druids may travel to these places to perform rituals, meditate, and connect with the energy and history of the land.

**Spiritual Quests**: Apart from physical travel, sacred journeys also encompass personal quests for wisdom and understanding. These can involve deep meditation, study, and engaging in practices that challenge and expand one's spiritual boundaries.

## Contemporary Expressions of Druidic Pilgrimages

In the modern context, Druidic pilgrimages have adapted to fit contemporary lifestyles and circumstances, yet they retain their core purpose of spiritual exploration and growth.

**Group Pilgrimages**: Organized pilgrimages where groups of Druids travel together are common. These group journeys offer a sense of community and shared experience, allowing participants to learn from each other and deepen their collective understanding of Druidic traditions.

**Solo Journeys**: Many modern Druids also undertake solo pilgrimages, seeking personal reflection and a deeper connection with the natural world. These journeys are often times of significant personal transformation and spiritual insight.

**Virtual Pilgrimages**: With the advent of digital technology, virtual pilgrimages have become a way for those unable to travel to experience sacred sites. Through online tours and interactive experiences, modern Druids can remotely connect with these significant places.

## The Impact of Sacred Journeys

The impact of sacred journeys in Druidry extends beyond the duration of the journey itself. These experiences often lead to profound personal growth, a deeper understanding of the interconnectedness of all life, and a renewed commitment to the Druid path.

**Personal Transformation**: Pilgrimages and quests often act as catalysts for personal change, helping individuals overcome challenges, gain new perspectives, and grow spiritually.

**Cultural and Historical Connection**: By visiting ancient sites and engaging in traditional practices, modern Druids forge a tangible connection with the past, enriching their understanding of Druidic history and culture.

**Ecological Awareness**: Through the deep connection with nature experienced during these journeys, many Druids develop a stronger commitment to ecological preservation and environmental activism.

Sacred journeys, whether physical pilgrimages or inner quests, are a vital aspect of modern Druidry, providing pathways for spiritual exploration, personal growth, and a deeper connection with the natural and spiritual worlds. These journeys, adapting to the needs and realities of the modern world, continue to be a cornerstone of the Druidic path, offering profound experiences of transformation and insight.

# CHAPTER 16: DRUIDIC COMMUNITIES AND ORDERS

In the tapestry of modern Druidry, communities and orders play a pivotal role in preserving traditions, fostering learning, and building a sense of kinship among practitioners. We examine the diverse landscape of Druidic communities and orders, including their structures, functions, and the unique roles they play in the contemporary Druidic movement.

## The Structure and Diversity of Druidic Communities

Druidic communities and orders vary widely in their structure, practices, and philosophies. Some are tightly-knit groups that focus on specific traditions or practices, while others are more eclectic, embracing a range of beliefs and rituals. The structure of these communities can be formal, with defined roles and hierarchies, or more fluid and egalitarian.

Key types of Druidic communities include:

**Groves**: These are local groups that often gather for rituals, celebrations, and learning. Groves may be affiliated with larger Druidic orders or operate independently, focusing on the needs and interests of their members.

**Orders**: These are larger organizations that often have a national or international presence. They provide a framework for Druidic practice, offering training programs, organizing events, and publishing materials on Druidry.

**Online Communities**: With the advent of the internet, virtual communities have become an integral part of modern Druidry. These platforms allow for the sharing of resources, discussion, and even virtual rituals, connecting Druids from all over the world.

## Functions and Activities of Druidic Communities

Druidic communities and orders serve several vital functions in the modern Druidic movement:

**Preservation and Transmission of Knowledge**: They are custodians of Druidic knowledge, preserving ancient wisdom and adapting it for contemporary practice. Through training programs, mentorship, and publications, they ensure that the teachings of Druidry are passed on to new generations.

**Spiritual and Ritual Practice**: Communities provide a space for collective rituals and celebrations, which are central to Druidic practice. These gatherings reinforce the communal bond and allow members to experience the power of group rituals.

**Support and Fellowship**: Druidic communities offer a sense of belonging and support. For many practitioners, these communities are a spiritual family where they can share experiences, learn from each other, and grow together in their spiritual paths.

## Challenges and Opportunities

Modern Druidic communities and orders face various challenges and opportunities in the 21st century:

**Inclusivity and Diversity**: As Druidry attracts a more diverse following, communities are challenged to be inclusive and accommodating of different perspectives and practices. This diversity can enrich the tradition, bringing in new ideas and approaches.

**Adapting to Change**: In a rapidly changing world, Druidic communities must find ways to stay relevant and accessible. This includes embracing technology, addressing contemporary issues, and evolving their practices while staying true to core principles.

**Environmental and Social Activism**: Many Druidic communities are actively involved in environmental and social causes, reflecting the Druidic reverence for nature and commitment to societal well-being. This activism is an expression of their spiritual values in action.

Druidic communities and orders are essential to the vitality and continuity of modern Druidry. They provide a framework for practice, a repository of knowledge, and a supportive network for practitioners. As they navigate the challenges of the modern world, these communities play a crucial role in shaping the future of the Druidic path, ensuring its relevance and vibrancy for generations to come.

## The Psychology of Druidic Rituals

The practice of Druidry, rich in rituals and ceremonies, is not only a spiritual journey but also a psychological one. We delve into the psychological aspects of Druidic rituals, exploring how they impact mental states, foster personal growth, and facilitate a deeper connection with the self and the natural world.

## Influence on Mental and Emotional States

Druidic rituals are designed to engage participants on multiple levels – physical, emotional, mental, and spiritual. This holistic engagement has profound psychological effects:

**Inducing Altered States of Consciousness**: Many Druidic rituals involve elements like rhythmic drumming, chanting, or meditative practices that can lead to altered states of consciousness. These states enable practitioners to transcend ordinary perception, accessing deeper levels of awareness and intuition.

**Emotional Catharsis**: Rituals often provide a safe space for the expression of emotions, allowing participants to process feelings like grief, joy, or gratitude more fully. This emotional release can be healing and transformative.

**Cognitive Reappraisal**: Engaging in rituals allows practitioners to reframe their perspectives on life events, fostering a sense of empowerment and resilience. Rituals often symbolize the cycle of life, death, and rebirth, offering new ways to understand and cope with change and loss.

## Personal Growth and Self-Reflection

Druidic rituals serve as catalysts for personal growth and self-reflection:

**Enhancing Self-Awareness**: The introspective nature of many Druidic practices encourages individuals to look inward, fostering greater self-awareness and understanding of one's thoughts, emotions, and behaviors.

**Promoting Mindfulness and Presence**: Druidry places a strong emphasis on being present in the moment, particularly in rituals that involve interaction with nature. This mindfulness practice enhances mental clarity, reduces stress, and improves overall well-being.

**Encouraging Integration of the Self**: Druidic rituals often involve symbolically traversing the realms of land, sea, and sky, or engaging with archetypal figures. These experiences can help individuals integrate different aspects of the self, leading to a more cohesive and balanced identity.

## Social and Collective Dimensions

Druidic rituals also have a significant social and collective dimension:

**Fostering Community and Belonging**: Participating in group rituals strengthens the sense of community and belonging. This social connection is crucial for mental health, providing support, validation, and a sense of shared purpose.

**Collective Effervescence**: Engaging in rituals with others can lead to a sense of collective effervescence – a shared euphoria that reinforces social bonds and communal identity. This experience is deeply rewarding and can enhance one's sense of interconnectedness with others and the world.

**Rituals as a Mode of Teaching and Learning**: In a communal setting, rituals serve as a powerful medium for transmitting values, traditions, and wisdom. This shared learning experience is not only educational but also builds a collective repository of knowledge and understanding.

The psychology of Druidic rituals is a complex and multifaceted area, interweaving the individual and the collective, the emotional and the cognitive, the spiritual and the mundane. These practices offer a rich tapestry of experiences that can profoundly impact mental and emotional well-being, personal growth, and social connectedness. By engaging in these rituals, modern Druids continue a tradition that nourishes the human psyche in ways that are as relevant today as they were in ancient times.

# CHAPTER 17: COMPARATIVE MYTHOLOGIES IN DRUIDRY

The exploration of mythology is a fundamental aspect of Druidic study, offering rich insights into the beliefs, values, and worldviews of ancient cultures. In this advanced exploration, we delve into the comparative analysis of Druidic mythology, examining its similarities and differences with other world mythologies, and the insights this comparison offers into the universal themes of human experience.

## Intersecting Themes in World Mythologies

Druidic mythology, deeply rooted in Celtic culture, shares several common themes with other mythological traditions:

**Creation and Cosmology**: Just as in many other cultures, Druidic myths often explore the origins of the world and the forces that shape it. Comparative study reveals similarities in how different cultures understand the cosmos, time, and the role of chaos and order in creation.

**Heroic Journeys and Quests**: The motif of the hero's journey, central in Celtic and Druidic tales, is also found in various other mythologies. These narratives often involve quests for knowledge, battles with formidable foes, and journeys to otherworldly realms, reflecting universal human experiences of struggle, growth, and transformation.

**Nature and the Divine**: Many mythologies, including the Druidic, personify natural elements as deities or spirits. This anthropomorphism highlights a shared human tendency to view nature as imbued with spiritual significance and reflects common beliefs about the interconnectedness of all life.

## Druidic Mythology in Comparative Perspective

When placed alongside other mythologies, certain unique aspects of Druidic mythology become apparent:

**Celtic Cycles of Myth**: Unlike the linear narratives seen in some cultures, Celtic myths often depict cyclical time, emphasizing regeneration and the interconnectedness of events. This perspective offers a unique understanding of time and existence.

**Emphasis on Otherworldly Realms**: Druidic myths frequently explore the concept of otherworldly realms, which are closely intertwined with the physical world. This contrasts with mythologies that depict a more distinct separation between the divine or spiritual realms and the earthly plane.

**Fluidity of Characters and Forms**: Celtic deities and mythological figures often display shape-shifting abilities and ambiguous qualities, reflecting a worldview that embraces complexity, transformation, and the blurring of boundaries.

## Insights from Comparative Mythology

Studying Druidic mythology in comparison with other traditions yields several insights:

**Cultural Exchange and Influence**: Comparative mythology

highlights the exchanges and influences between different cultures over time. For instance, similarities between Celtic and Norse mythologies can be traced back to historical interactions between these cultures.

**Universal Human Questions and Themes**: At their core, all mythologies grapple with the same fundamental human questions about creation, existence, morality, and the afterlife. This shared inquiry underscores the commonality of human experience across cultures and epochs.

**Adaptation and Evolution of Myths**: Understanding how Druidic myths compare with others also sheds light on how myths evolve and adapt over time, influenced by social, environmental, and historical contexts.

The comparative study of Druidic mythology offers a window into the rich tapestry of human belief and imagination. By exploring the similarities and differences with other mythological traditions, we gain a deeper appreciation of the universal themes that connect us and the unique perspectives that enrich our understanding of the world. This exploration not only deepens our knowledge of Druidry but also fosters a greater appreciation for the diversity and complexity of human cultural expression.

## Metaphysics and Druidry

In the advanced stages of Druidic study, metaphysics – the branch of philosophy that examines the fundamental nature of reality – plays a crucial role. We delve into the metaphysical principles underlying Druidic beliefs, exploring how these principles inform the Druidic understanding of the universe, life, and the interconnectedness of all things.

## Understanding the Druidic View of Reality

Druidic metaphysics is deeply rooted in a holistic view of the universe, where everything is interconnected and interdependent. This perspective is characterized by several key concepts:

**Immanence and Transcendence**: Druidry holds that the divine is both immanent, existing within all things, and transcendent, beyond the physical world. This dual aspect of the divine reflects a belief in the sacredness of the natural world as well as the existence of other realms or dimensions.

**Cycles of Nature and Existence**: A fundamental principle in Druidic thought is the cyclical nature of existence, mirrored in the changing seasons, life cycles, and even cosmic cycles. This perspective emphasizes the importance of balance, harmony, and the acceptance of change and transformation as natural processes.

**Interconnectivity of All Life**: Central to Druidic metaphysics is the idea that all life forms, including humans, animals, plants, and even inanimate objects, are connected in a complex web of relationships. This interconnectedness is seen as both physical and spiritual, with actions in one part of the web affecting the whole.

## Metaphysical Practices in Druidry

Druidic metaphysical concepts are not only theoretical but are also reflected in various practices:

**Meditation and Visualization**: Druids use meditation and visualization techniques to explore different levels of reality, connect with the natural world, and tap into deeper levels of consciousness.

**Ritual and Ceremony**: Druidic rituals often symbolize metaphysical concepts, such as the unity of the physical and spiritual, the cycle of birth, death, and rebirth, and the interconnectedness of all beings.

**Nature-based Practices**: Engaging with the natural world is a form of metaphysical practice in Druidry, helping to ground the abstract concepts of metaphysics in tangible experiences.

## The Implications of Druidic Metaphysics

The metaphysical principles of Druidry have profound implications for how Druids view and interact with the world:

**Ethical Considerations**: The belief in the sacredness of all life and the interconnectedness of all things informs Druidic ethical perspectives, emphasizing respect for nature, sustainability, and the importance of living in harmony with the earth.

**Spiritual Insight and Growth**: The metaphysical framework of Druidry offers a path for spiritual insight and growth, encouraging practitioners to explore the deeper mysteries of existence and their place in the universe.

**Healing and Restoration**: By understanding and aligning with the natural cycles and interconnected nature of reality, Druids engage in practices aimed at healing themselves, their communities, and the planet.

Metaphysics in Druidry provides a rich and complex framework for understanding the nature of reality and our place within it. These principles inform not just the philosophical aspects of Druidry but also its practical and ethical dimensions, guiding Druids in their pursuit of wisdom, harmony, and balance with the natural world.

# CHAPTER 18: ALCHEMY AND TRANSFORMATION IN DRUIDIC PRACTICES

Alchemy, traditionally known for the transmutation of base metals into gold, in Druidry, is understood in a more metaphysical and spiritual sense. Let's delve into the advanced concepts of spiritual alchemy and transformation within Druidic practices, exploring how these principles are applied for personal and collective growth.

## The Spiritual Alchemy in Druidry

In Druidry, alchemy is viewed as a transformative process of the self, where the practitioner undergoes a metaphorical journey from a base state to a more enlightened and refined existence. This process involves several stages:

**Purification and Preparation**: Similar to the alchemical concept of calcination, this stage involves the burning away of the ego and impurities, leading to a state of humility and readiness for transformation.

**Dissolution and Discovery**: In this phase, akin to alchemical dissolution, there is a breaking down of old structures and beliefs, allowing for the emergence of new insights and the discovery of inner truths.

**Reintegration and Rebirth**: Resembling alchemical coagulation, this stage represents the reintegration of these insights and truths into the individual's life, resulting in a rebirth of the self into a more harmonized and enlightened state.

## Transformation Through Druidic Rituals

Druidic rituals often symbolize and facilitate this alchemical transformation process:

**Seasonal Celebrations**: The eight festivals of the Druidic Wheel of the Year mark the cyclical nature of life and its constant state of flux and renewal, echoing the transformative journey of the soul.

**Rites of Passage**: These rituals, such as initiations into different grades (Bard, Ovate, and Druid), symbolize the stages of spiritual growth and the transformation of the practitioner's identity and role within the Druidic community.

**Nature-based Practices**: Engaging with the natural world in Druidry is seen as a way to connect with the cycles of growth, decay, and renewal, mirroring the inner alchemical process of the individual.

## Alchemy, Wisdom, and Enlightenment

The ultimate goal of spiritual alchemy in Druidry is to attain wisdom and enlightenment:

**Integration of Opposites**: The alchemical journey involves balancing and integrating opposing forces within the self, such as light and dark, masculine and feminine, physical and spiritual. This integration leads to a state of inner harmony and understanding.

**Attainment of Wisdom**: Through this transformative process, practitioners gain deeper wisdom, not just intellectually but also experientially, understanding the deeper truths of existence and their interconnectedness with all life.

**Service to the Community and the Earth**: The enlightened state in Druidic alchemy is not just for personal salvation but is also seen as a means to serve the community and the Earth. The wisdom gained is used to guide, heal, and nurture both society and the natural world.

Alchemy in Druidry represents a profound and intricate journey of spiritual transformation. It is a metaphorical process that involves purifying, discovering, and reintegrating aspects of the self, leading to a state of wisdom and enlightenment. This transformative path is central to the Druidic pursuit of personal growth and the harmonious balance with the natural world. Through this process, Druids seek not only personal fulfillment but also to contribute to the greater good of their community and the Earth.

## The Quantum Druid: Exploring the Intersection of Druidry and Quantum Physics

The intriguing intersection with quantum physics offers a contemporary perspective on ancient wisdom. Concepts from quantum physics resonate with Druidic teachings and practices, providing a deeper understanding of the nature of reality and our place within it.

## Quantum Concepts in Druidic Context

Quantum physics, with its focus on the behavior of the smallest particles in the universe, reveals a world that is profoundly interconnected and not entirely predictable, resonating deeply with Druidic views of nature and existence.

**Interconnectedness**: Quantum entanglement, where particles remain connected regardless of distance, echoes the Druidic principle of interconnectedness of all things in the universe. This concept underscores the belief that every action has an impact on the whole, a foundational idea in Druidic ethics and environmental consciousness.

**Observer Effect**: In quantum physics, the observer effect suggests that the act of observation influences the outcome of experiments. This parallels the Druidic idea that human consciousness interacts with and shapes the world around us, emphasizing the power of intention and perception in shaping reality.

**Potentiality and Manifestation**: Quantum physics introduces the concept of potentiality, where particles exist in multiple states simultaneously until observed. This aligns with Druidic beliefs in the power of potential and the manifestation of reality through intention, visualization, and ritual.

## Druidry in the Quantum Age

The alignment of quantum physics and Druidic principles offers a modern framework for understanding ancient wisdom:

**Redefining Magic**: The seemingly magical phenomena in quantum physics, such as particles being in two places at once, provide a scientific basis for reinterpreting what might be considered magical in Druidry. It allows a modern Druid to view magic as the interaction with the deeper, quantum level of reality.

**Ethical Implications**: Understanding the universe as an interconnected web, as both quantum physics and Druidry suggest, has profound ethical implications. It fosters a worldview that emphasizes responsibility for our actions and their impacts on the broader ecosystem.

**Ritual and Practice**: The parallels between quantum mechanics and Druidic practice can enrich ritual work, infusing it with a deeper understanding of how intention and consciousness might interact with the fabric of reality.

## Challenges and Opportunities

Integrating quantum physics into Druidic practice is not without challenges, yet it offers exciting opportunities:

**Complexity and Mystery**: Quantum physics is inherently complex and often counterintuitive, mirroring the mysteries at the heart of Druidic practice. Embracing this complexity can deepen the sense of awe and wonder in Druidic practice.

**Dialogue Between Science and Spirituality**: This intersection opens up a dialogue between science and spirituality, challenging and expanding our understanding of both fields. It invites a more holistic view of the world that harmonizes scientific understanding with spiritual wisdom.

**Personal and Collective Growth**: Incorporating insights from quantum physics into Druidry can aid personal growth and development, offering new perspectives on the nature of reality, consciousness, and our potential to effect change.

The intersection of Druidry and quantum physics offers a rich and fertile ground for exploration. It bridges ancient wisdom with modern science, providing a unique perspective on the mysteries of the universe and our role within it. This convergence invites Druids to explore new dimensions of understanding, ethics, and practice, fostering a deeper connection with the natural world and the unseen forces that shape our reality.

# CHAPTER 19: THE PHILOSOPHER'S STONE: WISDOM IN DRUIDRY

Let's explore the concept of the Philosopher's Stone, not as a literal substance for transmuting base metals into gold, but as a metaphor for wisdom and enlightenment in Druidic practices. This advanced exploration delves into the transformative journey towards wisdom, the role of nature in this process, and the application of this wisdom in daily life.

## The Transformative Journey to Wisdom

In Druidry, the quest for the Philosopher's Stone is akin to the pursuit of deep, spiritual wisdom. This journey involves several key aspects:

**Self-Discovery and Inner Alchemy**: Just as the alchemist seeks to transform lead into gold, the Druid seeks to transform the self. This involves introspection, meditation, and confronting one's shadows, leading to personal growth and spiritual awakening.

**Integration of Knowledge and Experience**: True wisdom in Druidry comes from the integration of intellectual knowledge with personal experience. It is about understanding the cycles of nature, the flow of the seasons, and the rhythms of life, and incorporating this understanding into one's worldview.

**Ethical Living and Wisdom**: Druidic wisdom is not only about personal enlightenment but also involves ethical living. It teaches balance, harmony with nature, and responsibility for one's actions, reflecting a deep understanding of the interconnectedness of all things.

## The Role of Nature in Attaining Wisdom

Nature plays a central role in the Druidic path to wisdom:

**Learning from the Natural World**: Druids believe that nature is a teacher and a guide. The patterns and cycles of nature offer insights into the nature of existence and our place within the larger web of life.

**Rituals and Ceremonies**: Druidic rituals, often conducted in natural settings, are designed to align practitioners with the natural world, opening pathways to deeper understanding and wisdom.

**The Healing Power of Nature**: Engaging with nature is also seen as a healing process, helping to restore balance and clarity, which are essential for the development of wisdom.

## Application of Wisdom in Daily Life

Druidic wisdom is not meant to be esoteric or detached from everyday life. Instead, it has practical applications:

**Living in Harmony with Nature**: Wisdom in Druidry encourages sustainable living, respecting and protecting the environment, and understanding our role as stewards of the Earth.

**Community and Relationships**: Wisdom extends to understanding and nurturing relationships, recognizing the importance of community, and practicing compassion and empathy.

**Personal Fulfillment and Service**: The ultimate goal of attaining wisdom in Druidry is to achieve personal fulfillment and to serve others. It is about using one's knowledge and experience to contribute to the well-being of others and the world.

The pursuit of the Philosopher's Stone in Druidry symbolizes the journey to wisdom and enlightenment. This wisdom is deeply rooted in understanding and living in harmony with nature, integrating knowledge and experience, and applying these insights in ethical and meaningful ways. It is a journey of transformation, not just of the self but also of the world around us, embodying the true essence of Druidic spirituality.

## Sacred Sound and Vibrational Healing

Let's explore the concepts of sacred sound and vibrational healing in Druidry by delving into the ancient and modern understanding of sound's power in healing practices, the role of music and chant in Druidic rituals, and the integration of these practices into contemporary Druidic spirituality.

## The Power of Sound in Druidic Practices

Sound has always been an integral part of Druidic rituals and practices, believed to possess profound healing properties and the ability to connect the physical and spiritual realms.

**Vibrational Nature of Sound**: Druids understand that sound is vibration and that these vibrations can interact with the energetic fields of living beings. This interaction can bring about changes in physical, emotional, and spiritual well-being.

**Use of Chants and Songs**: Traditional Druidic chants and songs are more than mere words set to melody; they are considered tools for transformation. These sounds are thought to resonate with specific energies of nature and the cosmos, harmonizing the individual's energy with these larger forces.

**Instruments in Rituals**: Instruments such as drums, flutes, and harps are often used in Druidic rituals. The rhythmic beating of a drum, for example, is used to induce trance states, facilitate meditation, and connect with the deeper rhythms of nature.

## Integration of Sound Healing in Modern Druidry

As Druidry evolves, the use of sound and vibrational healing has adapted to incorporate contemporary understanding and techniques:

**Sound Baths and Healing Sessions**: Modern Druids may conduct sound baths, where participants are immersed in the sounds of gongs, singing bowls, and other instruments, facilitating deep relaxation and healing.

**Chanting and Mantra Meditation**: The use of chanting, drawing from both traditional Druidic and other spiritual traditions, has become a common practice. Chanting mantras can help focus the mind, elevate the spirit, and harness personal and universal energies.

**Nature Sounds for Healing**: Recognizing the restorative power of nature's sounds, such as the rustling of leaves, flowing water, or bird calls, modern Druids often integrate these sounds into meditation and healing practices.

## The Role of Sound in Spiritual Growth and Community

The use of sound and vibrational healing extends beyond personal well-being and plays a significant role in Druidic spiritual growth and community bonding:

**Enhancing Spiritual Experiences**: Sacred sound is used to deepen spiritual experiences, facilitate journeying to other realms, and connect with deities or ancestral spirits in rituals and ceremonies.

**Community Building**: Group singing and music-making in Druidic gatherings are not just for enjoyment; they are essential for building community bonds and creating a shared energetic space.

**Ecological Connection**: Sound practices in Druidry also foster a deeper connection with the natural world. Listening to and creating sounds that reflect nature's rhythms encourages a harmonious relationship with the environment.

Sacred sound and vibrational healing are key components of advanced Druidic practices. These practices offer profound healing benefits, enhance spiritual experiences, and strengthen the bonds within the Druidic community and with the natural world. By integrating traditional wisdom with modern techniques, Druids continue to explore and experience the transformative power of sound.

# CHAPTER 20:
# ASTRAL TRAVEL AND OTHERWORLDLY REALMS

We will investigate the advanced Druidic practices of astral travel and the exploration of otherworldly realms, including the concepts and techniques for navigating these spiritual journeys, the significance of otherworldly experiences in Druidic tradition, and the integration of these experiences into personal spiritual growth.

## Understanding Astral Travel in Druidry

Astral travel, or astral projection, is a practice where the consciousness separates from the physical body to journey in the astral plane. In Druidry, this practice is deeply rooted in the belief in otherworldly realms and the interconnectedness of all existence.

**Techniques and Preparation**: Successful astral travel in Druidic practice often involves deep meditation, visualization, and ritual preparation. Techniques may include focusing on specific symbols, rhythmic breathing, and the use of chants or mantras to achieve the necessary state of consciousness.

**Safety and Grounding**: Emphasis is placed on the importance of grounding and protecting oneself before attempting astral travel. This includes practices for energy shielding and methods for ensuring a safe return to the physical body.

**Ethical Considerations**: Druidic teachings stress the ethical implications of astral travel, emphasizing respect for all beings encountered and the integrity of one's actions in the astral realm.

## Exploring Otherworldly Realms

The concept of otherworldly realms is central to Druidic cosmology, with these realms being seen as places of deep wisdom, learning, and connection with the divine.

**The Nature of the Realms**: Druidic tradition describes various realms, each with its unique characteristics and inhabitants. These include realms of ancestors, spirit guides, and deities, as well as elemental and nature spirits.

**Learning and Guidance**: Journeys to these realms are often sought for wisdom, healing, and spiritual guidance. Interactions with otherworldly beings can provide insights into personal challenges, spiritual development, and deeper universal truths.

**Integration of Experiences**: Experiences in these realms are believed to offer profound personal transformations. Druids seek to integrate these experiences into their daily lives, using the insights gained to enhance their understanding, compassion, and connection to the natural world.

## The Role of Astral Travel in Modern Druidry

In contemporary Druidic practice, astral travel continues to be a vital aspect of spiritual exploration and growth.

**Personal Development**: Astral travel is seen as a tool for personal growth, self-discovery, and the expansion of one's consciousness beyond the physical realm.

**Community and Teaching**: Experiences in astral travel are often shared within the Druidic community, contributing to a collective understanding and the passing down of wisdom.

**Adapting Ancient Practices to Modern Times**: Modern Druids adapt ancient techniques of astral travel to contemporary practices, blending traditional wisdom with new insights and understandings.

Astral travel and the exploration of otherworldly realms are advanced practices in Druidry that offer profound spiritual experiences. These journeys allow practitioners to transcend the physical world, gain wisdom and guidance from other realms, and integrate these experiences into their spiritual path. By engaging in these practices, modern Druids continue a tradition of exploration and connection that is as relevant today as it was in ancient times.

## The Ethics and Morality of Modern Druidry

We will explore how Druids today interpret and apply ancient principles to contemporary ethical dilemmas, the role of nature-centric ethics, and the importance of personal responsibility and community in moral decision-making.

## Contemporary Interpretation of Ancient Principles

Modern Druidry, while rooted in ancient traditions, faces new ethical challenges in today's world. The adaptation of ancient Druidic principles to contemporary issues is a key aspect of ethical practice in modern Druidry.

**Relevance of Ancient Wisdom**: Druids look to their ancient past for guidance on living ethically, interpreting age-old wisdom in the context of modern societal and environmental challenges.

**The Druidic Virtues**: Principles such as truth, honor, and integrity, which were esteemed in ancient Druidry, are adapted to guide behavior in areas like environmental stewardship, social justice, and personal conduct.

**Balancing Tradition and Modernity**: The challenge for modern Druids lies in balancing reverence for tradition with the need to address current global issues, from climate change to social inequality.

## Nature-Centric Ethics in Druidry

At the heart of Druidic ethics is a profound respect for nature, which informs moral decision-making and actions.

**Environmental Stewardship**: Druidry advocates for living in harmony with the Earth, encouraging sustainable practices and environmental activism.

**Interconnectedness and Responsibility**: Recognizing the interconnectedness of all life, Druids feel a moral responsibility to protect ecosystems and biodiversity.

**Learning from Nature**: Druids believe that observing natural systems can offer insights into ethical living, such as the importance of balance, diversity, and symbiosis.

## Personal Responsibility and Community

Druidic ethics emphasize both personal responsibility and the role of community in cultivating a moral society.

**Individual Ethics**: Each Druid is encouraged to develop a personal code of ethics, reflecting on how their actions align with Druidic principles and affect the broader world.

**Community and Cultural Ethics**: Druidic communities often engage in discussions about ethics, providing a space for collective reflection, learning, and support in ethical practices.

**Service to Others**: Druidry teaches that ethical living includes service to others, fostering a sense of community, kinship, and mutual aid.

## Challenges in Ethical Druidry

Modern Druids face unique challenges in applying their ethics in a complex world.

**Navigating Modern Dilemmas**: Issues such as technology use, political involvement, and global economics require Druids to constantly reassess and redefine their ethical stances.

**Diversity within Druidry**: As a diverse and evolving spiritual path, Druidry encompasses a wide range of perspectives, leading to rich but sometimes challenging ethical debates within the community.

**Global and Local Action**: Druids are called to act ethically on both global and local scales, balancing immediate community needs with broader environmental and societal concerns.

The ethics and morality of modern Druidry are dynamic and evolving, rooted in ancient wisdom but responsive to contemporary challenges. Through a deep connection with nature, a commitment to personal and communal responsibility, and an ongoing dialogue within the community, Druids seek to live ethically and contribute positively to the world. This chapter underscores the importance of ethical living as a cornerstone of Druidic practice and its relevance in today's increasingly complex world.

# CHAPTER 21: THE DRUID'S PATH TO SELF-MASTERY

Let's examine the concept of self-mastery within the context of modern Druidry. It explores how Druids cultivate personal growth, self-awareness, and mastery over their internal and external environments through spiritual practices, ethical living, and a deep connection with nature.

## Cultivating Personal Growth and Self-Awareness

In Druidry, the journey towards self-mastery is a lifelong process of personal development that involves understanding and harmonizing the self with the natural world and the wider community.

**Self-Reflection and Meditation**: Integral to self-mastery in Druidry is the practice of self-reflection and meditation. These practices aid in understanding one's thoughts, emotions, and actions, leading to greater self-awareness and mindfulness.

**Balancing the Inner and Outer Worlds**: Druids strive to achieve balance between their inner selves and the external world. This includes harmonizing personal desires and ambitions with the needs of the community and the environment.

**Continuous Learning and Adaptation**: Self-mastery involves an ongoing commitment to learning, growing, and adapting. Druids view life as a continuous journey of discovery, where each experience provides an opportunity for personal development.

## Ethical Living as a Path to Self-Mastery

Ethical conduct is a cornerstone of the Druidic path to self-mastery. Living in accordance with Druidic values and principles is seen as essential to personal growth and spiritual fulfillment.

**Living in Harmony with Nature**: Druids believe that ethical living involves a deep respect for and harmony with nature. This includes sustainable living, environmental stewardship, and recognizing the interconnectedness of all life.

**Community Involvement and Service**: Engaging with and serving one's community is viewed as a vital part of self-mastery. Druids often participate in community service, social justice initiatives, and efforts to support and uplift others.

**Personal Responsibility and Integrity**: Druidry teaches that personal responsibility and integrity are key to self-mastery. This means being accountable for one's actions, living truthfully, and upholding one's commitments and responsibilities.

## Practices for Self-Mastery in Modern Druidry

Modern Druidry offers a range of practices and rituals that support the journey to self-mastery.

**Ritual and Ceremony**: Regular participation in Druidic rituals and ceremonies helps to reinforce personal commitment to the path of self-mastery. These rituals often involve affirmations of intention, gratitude, and the celebration of personal growth.

**Nature Connection**: Spending time in nature and engaging in practices such as forest bathing, wildlife observation, and gardening are seen as vital for grounding and connecting with the

Earth, which is central to self-mastery in Druidry.

**Creative Expression**: Many Druids use creative expression, such as writing, art, and music, as tools for self-discovery and personal growth. These creative practices are avenues for exploring and expressing the inner self.

The Druid's path to self-mastery is a multifaceted journey that encompasses personal growth, ethical living, and a deep connection with nature. Through self-reflection, community engagement, and spiritual practice, modern Druids strive to master themselves and in doing so, contribute positively to their communities and the natural world. This underscores the importance of self-mastery in Druidic spirituality and its relevance in today's world.

## Shamanic Practices in Modern Druidry

Let's delve into the integration and adaptation of shamanic practices within modern Druidry and explore the historical connections between Druidry and shamanism, the incorporation of shamanic elements into contemporary Druidic practices, and the role of these practices in personal and communal spiritual development.

## Historical Connections and Contemporary Perspectives

Shamanic elements have been intertwined with Druidic practices historically, both sharing a deep reverence for nature and the use of altered states of consciousness for spiritual exploration.

**Historical Overlap**: Ancient Druids, like shamans, were seen as mediators between the physical and spiritual worlds. They used trance, divination, and ritual to gain insights and guide their communities.

**Modern Adaptation**: Contemporary Druids often draw on

shamanic techniques such as journeying, animal totems, and drumming, adapting them within a Druidic framework to enhance spiritual practice.

**Respecting Cultural Origins**: Modern Druids are mindful of the cultural origins of shamanic practices, approaching them with respect and acknowledging their diverse global sources.

## Shamanic Elements in Druidic Rituals

Shamanic practices are incorporated into Druidic rituals to deepen the connection with the natural world and the spiritual realm.

**Drumming and Trance Work**: Drumming is commonly used in Druidic rituals to induce trance states, facilitating journeys to otherworldly realms and deepening meditation practices.

**Animal Spirits and Totems**: Many Druids work with animal spirits as guides and protectors, seeing them as messengers and teachers that offer wisdom and insight.

**Nature Connection**: Shamanic practices emphasize a profound connection with nature, encouraging Druids to engage deeply with the land, plants, and animals as part of their spiritual path.

## Personal and Communal Development Through Shamanic Practices

Shamanic elements in Druidry contribute to both personal growth and the strengthening of community bonds.

**Personal Transformation**: Shamanic journeying and meditation offer pathways for self-discovery, healing, and personal transformation, allowing individuals to explore their subconscious and spiritual dimensions.

**Community Healing and Support**: Shamanic practices in

Druidry often include group rituals and ceremonies that foster community healing, support, and a shared sense of spiritual purpose.

**Ecological Awareness**: Engaging with shamanic practices heightens ecological awareness and responsibility, aligning with the Druidic emphasis on environmental stewardship and sustainability.

## Challenges and Ethical Considerations

Integrating shamanic practices into modern Druidry also presents certain challenges and ethical considerations.

**Cultural Sensitivity**: Druids are aware of the need for cultural sensitivity and avoiding appropriation when incorporating shamanic practices from other traditions.

**Balancing Tradition and Innovation**: Finding a balance between traditional Druidic practices and the incorporation of shamanic elements can be challenging, requiring a thoughtful approach that respects the integrity of both paths.

**Accessibility and Inclusivity**: Ensuring that shamanic-influenced practices are accessible and inclusive to all members of the Druid community is a key consideration, promoting diversity and understanding within the tradition.

This highlights the valuable role of shamanic practices in modern Druidry, contributing to the richness and depth of Druidic spiritual practice. By incorporating shamanic elements, modern Druids embrace a holistic approach to spirituality that honors their ancestral roots while adapting to the needs and understandings of the contemporary world.

# CHAPTER 22: THEURGY AND DIVINE CONTACT

We will explore the advanced practice of Theurgy within modern Druidry, focusing on establishing contact with divine energies and being whilst exploring the nature of Theurgy, methods to connect with the divine, and the role of divine contact in Druidic practices.

## Understanding Theurgy in Modern Druidry

Theurgy in Druidry is the practice of invoking the presence of divine forces or deities for spiritual development and transformation.

**Concept of Theurgy**: Theurgy in Druidry is understood as a sacred process of aligning with divine energies to enhance spiritual growth and understanding. It goes beyond mere ritual to create a profound connection with the spiritual realm.

**Divine as a Source of Inspiration and Wisdom**: Druids view divine contact not as a means for material gain but as a pathway to gain wisdom, inspiration, and insight. This contact is sought to deepen one's spiritual practice and understanding of the universe.

**Integrating Theurgy with Druidic Beliefs**: Theurgy in Druidry is seamlessly integrated with its core beliefs, such as reverence for nature, the sanctity of life, and the interconnectedness of all things.

## Methods of Establishing Divine Contact

Druids use various methods to establish contact with divine energies, each tailored to individual beliefs and experiences.

**Ritual and Ceremony**: Specialized rituals and ceremonies are conducted to invoke divine presences. These often involve specific chants, offerings, and symbolic actions designed to align the practitioner with the energies being invoked.

**Meditation and Visualization**: Meditation and visualization are key practices in Theurgy. Druids meditate to reach a state of consciousness where they can perceive and interact with divine energies.

**Nature-Based Practices**: As Druidry is deeply connected with nature, many Druids find divine contact through interactions with the natural world, seeing the divine in every aspect of the natural environment.

## The Role of Divine Contact in Druidic Practice

Divine contact plays a significant role in the spiritual lives of Druids, influencing both their personal practices and their contributions to their communities.

**Personal Transformation**: Engaging with divine energies is seen as a catalyst for personal transformation and spiritual enlightenment. It is a deeply personal journey that varies from one individual to another.

**Community and Cultural Impact**: Divine contact also influences the way Druids interact with their communities. Insights gained from these experiences often guide Druids in their roles as healers, teachers, and leaders.

**Ethical Considerations and Challenges**: The practice of Theurgy comes with its ethical considerations. Druids approach these practices with humility and respect, acknowledging the limits of human understanding in the face of the divine.

Theurgy and divine contact in modern Druidry represent a profound and complex aspect of the Druidic spiritual path. This practice allows Druids to explore the deeper realms of spirituality, providing insights and experiences that enrich their understanding of the universe and their place within it. Through Theurgy, Druids seek not only personal enlightenment but also to contribute to the greater good of their communities and the world at large.

## Sacred Sexuality in Druidry

Let's investigate the complex and profound subject of sacred sexuality within Druidry and examine the historical context, the spiritual significance, and the contemporary practices of sacred sexuality in the Druidic tradition.

## Historical Context and Evolution

Sacred sexuality in Druidry has ancient roots, intertwining with Celtic myths and rituals. Historically, sexuality was revered as a potent force of nature and creation.

**Ancient Beliefs**: In ancient Druidic culture, sexuality was often linked with fertility rites and the natural cycles of the Earth. It was a means to honor the divine and the life-giving forces of nature.

**Evolution Over Centuries**: Over time, the interpretation and practice of sacred sexuality have evolved. Modern Druidry reinterprets these ancient practices with a contemporary understanding of sexuality, consent, and spiritual connection.

## Spiritual Significance

In Druidry, sexuality is not merely a physical act but a profound spiritual experience that connects individuals to the divine and the natural world.

**Connection with Nature**: Sexual union is seen as a mirror of the natural processes of creation and regeneration, symbolizing the interconnectedness of all life.

**Energetic Exchange**: Sacred sexuality is considered an exchange of energy that can lead to heightened spiritual awareness and deeper understanding of one's own divine nature.

**Tool for Personal and Spiritual Growth**: It is also a path for personal growth and spiritual development, allowing individuals to explore the depths of their being and their connection to the universe.

## Contemporary Practices and Ethics

Modern Druidic practitioners approach sacred sexuality with mindfulness, emphasizing consent, respect, and spiritual intention.

**Consensual and Respectful Practices**: Modern Druids advocate for consensual and respectful expressions of sexuality, with a strong emphasis on the physical, emotional, and spiritual well-being of all participants.

**Ritual and Ceremony**: Sacred sexuality is often incorporated into rituals and ceremonies, creating a sacred space where sexuality is expressed as a form of divine worship and connection.

**Integration with Other Spiritual Practices**: It is integrated with meditation, energy work, and other spiritual practices to create a holistic approach to spirituality that honors the sacredness of the sexual self.

In Druidry, sacred sexuality is a profound and integral part of the spiritual path. It is a practice that honors the divine within and around us, connecting deeply with the rhythms of nature and the universe. By embracing the sacredness of sexuality, Druids explore the depths of their spirituality and forge a stronger connection with the natural world and the divine.

# CHAPTER 23: ADVANCED MAGICAL SYSTEMS AND THEOREMS IN DRUIDRY

Next, we explore the intricate and advanced magical systems and theorems that form a part of contemporary Druidic practice and provide an insight into the complex mathematical and theoretical frameworks that underpin the mystical practices within Druidry.

## Theoretical Foundations of Druidic Magic

In Druidry, magical practices are not only seen as rituals but also as sophisticated systems with deep theoretical underpinnings.

**Mathematical Symbolism**: Numbers and geometric patterns are seen as fundamental to understanding the universe. Druidic magic often incorporates these elements to create symbolic representations of natural laws and cosmic order.

**Theoretical Constructs**: Concepts such as the interconnectedness of all beings, the flow of energy in the universe, and the impact of intention on reality are central to Druidic magical theory. These constructs provide a framework for understanding how magic operates within the natural world.

## Advanced Magical Systems

Druidry includes a variety of advanced magical systems, each with its own unique practices and philosophical basis.

**Ogham-Based Magic**: Building upon the ancient Druidic alphabet, Ogham, this system uses symbolic language to interact with the natural world and the energies it contains.

**Astronomical Alignments**: Druids study and utilize the alignments of celestial bodies for timing and enhancing their magical workings, believing that these alignments have profound effects on energy flow and consciousness.

**Elemental Magic**: Advanced elemental practices involve not only the four traditional elements (earth, air, fire, water) but also consider the quintessence or spirit, delving into the deeper metaphysical aspects of each element.

## Integration of Magic and Science

Modern Druidry often seeks to integrate magical practice with scientific understanding, seeing them as complementary rather than contradictory.

**Quantum Theories**: Some Druidic practitioners explore parallels between quantum physics and magical practice, particularly in concepts such as the observer effect, interconnectedness, and the nature of reality.

**Eco-Magic**: This approach combines ecological science with magical practice, using ritual to positively influence the environment and promote ecological balance and sustainability.

Advanced magical systems in Druidry represent a harmonious blend of ancient wisdom and modern understanding. These systems are deeply rooted in the natural world, reflecting a profound respect for the universe and its laws. By studying and applying these advanced systems and theorems, Druids engage in a continuous process of learning and spiritual growth, contributing to their journey towards wisdom and enlightenment.

## The Future of Druidry

Let's embark on an explorative journey into the potential future pathways and evolutions of Druidry by delving into the prospective trends, challenges, and advancements that might shape the Druidic path in the years to come.

## Technological Integration and Evolution

As we move further into the digital age, Druidry, like many other spiritual paths, faces the challenge and opportunity of integrating technology into its practices.

**Digital Ritual Spaces**: The potential for virtual gatherings and rituals through advanced technology, allowing practitioners from all over the world to participate in ceremonies and sacred observances.

**Eco-Technological Synergy**: The growing importance of eco-friendly technologies in Druidic practice, emphasizing the harmonious relationship between nature and technology to promote environmental sustainability.

## Societal Influence and Growth

Druidry's role within the broader societal context is likely to expand, addressing contemporary global challenges.

**Environmental Advocacy**: Druids are expected to take on more significant roles as advocates for environmental protection and sustainability, leveraging their spiritual connection to nature to drive ecological initiatives.

**Cultural Influence**: As interest in spiritual and earth-centered practices grows, Druidry may influence various aspects of culture, from art and music to community building and social activism.

## Theoretical and Philosophical Expansions

Druidic philosophy and its theoretical framework are anticipated to evolve, integrating new insights and discoveries from various fields.

**Quantum Mysticism**: The interplay between Druidic practices and quantum physics could lead to new understandings of reality and spirituality, offering a unique perspective on the interconnectedness of all existence.

**Global Druidic Synthesis**: The potential for synthesizing Druidic wisdom with other spiritual traditions from around the world, leading to a more inclusive and diverse spiritual practice.

As we look to the future of Druidry, it is clear that the path is dynamic and evolving. While staying true to its roots in nature and ancient wisdom, Druidry is poised to adapt and grow in response to the changing world. The future of Druidry is not just about preserving the past but also about forging new pathways and integrating new insights for a sustainable, harmonious, and spiritually fulfilling future.

# CHAPTER 24: SYNCRETISM AND THE GLOBAL DRUID

As the sun sets on the horizon of our comprehensive exploration of Druidry, we arrive at a compelling facet of this ancient path: its syncretism and global influence. Let's delve into how Druidry, while deeply rooted in its Celtic origins, has embraced and integrated elements from various spiritual paths and cultures, evolving into a truly global phenomenon.

## The Interweaving of Traditions

Druidry, traditionally seen through the lens of ancient Celtic spirituality, has always been a fluid and adaptable path. In the modern era, this adaptability has allowed it to intersect with diverse spiritual practices and philosophies. This syncretism is not a dilution of its essence but an enrichment that brings a more holistic and inclusive approach to spirituality.

**Integration with Eastern Philosophies**: The modern Druid path has shown a remarkable affinity for integrating concepts from Eastern philosophies such as Buddhism and Hinduism. Concepts like mindfulness, meditation, and a deeper understanding of the self and the universe have found resonance within Druidic practices.

**Influence of Western Esotericism**: Elements of Western esoteric traditions, including Kabbalah and Hermeticism, have also woven their way into Druidry, offering new dimensions of mystical understanding and magical practice.

**Embracing Indigenous Wisdom**: There's been a growing appreciation and incorporation of indigenous wisdom from around the world, recognizing the shared reverence for nature and the wisdom of ancestors.

## Druidry in a Global Context

The expansion of Druidry beyond its Celtic roots into a global movement has been a journey of both challenges and opportunities. This global spread has brought about a cross-pollination of ideas, practices, and perspectives, enriching the path for all who walk it.

**Cultural Sensitivity and Adaptation**: As Druidry spreads, it faces the challenge of respectfully integrating practices from various cultures. This requires a deep sensitivity and understanding to avoid cultural appropriation and to honor the origins and contexts of these practices.

**Building Global Communities**: The digital age has facilitated the growth of international Druidic communities. These online platforms have become spaces for shared learning, support, and the celebration of the diversity within the Druidic world.

**Eco-Spirituality as a Universal Language**: The environmental focus of Druidry has found a universal appeal. As our planet faces ecological crises, the Druidic emphasis on living in harmony with nature resonates across cultures, making it a truly global concern and connecting point.

## The Path Ahead: Syncretism as Evolution

The journey of Druidry into the future is marked by its continued evolution through syncretism. This evolutionary process is not about losing its identity but about enriching its tapestry with diverse threads of human spiritual experience.

**Honoring the Roots, Embracing the New**: As Druidry grows, it continues to honor its Celtic roots while also embracing new influences. This balance is key to maintaining its integrity and relevance.

**A Living Tradition**: Druidry, as a living tradition, adapts and evolves with time. This dynamism ensures that it remains a vibrant and meaningful path for seekers in the modern world.

**Unity in Diversity**: The syncretism of Druidry is a testament to its underlying philosophy of unity in diversity. It acknowledges that while paths may differ, the quest for understanding, connection, and harmony with the natural world is a shared human endeavor.

As Druidry stands at the crossroads of the ancient and the modern, the local and the global, it continues to offer a rich, diverse, and evolving path of spiritual practice. Its journey is a beacon of hope and unity, demonstrating that wisdom and reverence for nature transcend cultural and geographical boundaries.

In the serene embrace of ancient woods, under the watchful gaze of the moon, and in the harmonious chorus of nature, we find the spirit of Druidry alive and thriving. As we draw this book to a close, let us reflect on the journey we have traversed together, exploring the depths of Druidic resurgence and its manifestation in the modern world.

## The Timeless Tapestry of Druidry

Druidry, an ancient path, steeped in mystery and wisdom, has shown us the importance of living in harmony with nature.

It has taught us to revere the Earth, honor the cycles of the Wheel of the Year, and to find spiritual connection in the land, our ancestors, and the cosmos. This journey through the chapters has been a testament to the enduring relevance of these principles. We've rediscovered how the old ways, though ancient, resonate profoundly in our contemporary lives, offering solace, understanding, and a deep, abiding connection to all that is.

## The Evolution of Modern Druidry

The modern Druidic movement, a vibrant tapestry of diverse threads, has been a story of rebirth and adaptation. From the misty hills of ancient Celtic lands to the digital forums of the internet age, Druidry has evolved to embrace a global community. We've witnessed its journey from a localized tradition to a worldwide spiritual path, open to all who seek its wisdom. This evolution is not just a change in numbers but a profound expansion in perspectives, practices, and interpretations.

**Embracing Diversity**: Druidry today celebrates the multitude of voices within its fold. It's a path where different cultures, beliefs, and practices converge, each adding their unique hue to the Druidic spectrum.

**Eco-Spiritual Awakening**: Amidst the environmental challenges of our time, Druidry has emerged as a beacon of eco-consciousness. We have seen how its principles inspire a deeper ecological understanding and an active engagement in environmental stewardship.

**Communal Bonds**: The essence of community in Druidry, both in physical groves and online sanctuaries, has been a source of strength and inspiration. These communal bonds have fostered a sense of belonging, shared learning, and collective celebration.

## Envisioning the Future Path

As we look towards the horizon, the future of Druidry shimmers with potential. It invites us to continue exploring, adapting, and growing within this ancient yet ever-new tradition.

**The Journey Continues**: The path of Druidry is endless, with each step offering deeper insights and more profound experiences. We are encouraged to keep learning, practicing, and evolving on this spiritual journey.

**Innovation and Tradition**: As Druidry walks into the future, it balances the preservation of ancient wisdom with the incorporation of new ideas and technologies. This dynamic equilibrium ensures that the path remains relevant and vibrant.

**Heritage and Progress**: The commitment to preserving the core traditions of Druidry while embracing the changes of the modern era is paramount. This delicate balance ensures that the essence of Druidry, its heart, and soul, is passed on to future generations intact yet enriched.

## Final Reflections

As we conclude this exploration, let us carry forward the wisdom, experiences, and connections we have forged. Druidry, a path of harmony, wisdom, and deep ecological insight, offers a unique lens through which to view our world and our place within it. It is a journey of continuous discovery, a path that weaves together the past, present, and future into a tapestry of spiritual fulfillment.

In the spirit of Druidry, let us walk forth with reverence for nature, a thirst for knowledge, and a heart full of gratitude for the journey. The path is ever-unfolding, and each of us is a pilgrim on this sacred journey of rediscovery and resurgence.

# THE END

Printed in Dunstable, United Kingdom

72481499R00076